187 Kilometres, turn left

To Sheila,

I'm very jealous!

187 Kilometres, turn left

A New Zealand adventure via Australia and Singapore

By C.L. Peache

clpeache x

187 Kilometres, turn left

ISBN: 9798614530396

Copyright © C.L. Peache 2020

All rights reserved, including the right to reproduce the content in any form. No part of this publication shall be reproduced in any form without the express written consent of the author.

Independently published, available in paperback or e-book.

Cover design by Christine Goldschmidt

Typesetting by narrator
narrator.me.uk
info@narrator.me.uk
033 022 300 39

Dedications and Acknowledgements

To my mum, who is my biggest champion in life. I couldn't do any of this without your support and encouragement.

To my dad, I wish you were here to see my journey.

To you both for being the best parents a lass could ask for.

To Chris, thank you for the memories and many more to come.

Thank you to everyone who has helped me to turn this journal into a book. I really could not have done it without you. Special thanks to Maria for the editing, Christine Goldschmidt for the beautiful cover, Ash, Bonnie, Jane, Janice, Karla, Ric, Tracey, and of course my Mum and brothers for being my wonderful beta readers.
(If I've missed anyone, I'm SO sorry!)

Part One: Singapore

Setting off
Day 1 | Monday 18th February

After spending the morning panicking when I realise that all our holiday clothes don't fit in the cases… Oops! I take out a few bits and add them to our ever-increasing rucksacks. The idea was not to have heavy rucksacks. My back is playing up after I pulled a muscle doing a skydive in October 2018 and my Other Half; Chris has general wear and tear, he's also pushing 50, and part of the reason for this trip. I won't go on about the possible mid-life crisis I'm not acknowledging. But we're definitely not going to be the kind of people you see hitchhiking at the side of the road; figures barely discernible as humans due to the size of the backpacks attached to the front and back of their bodies. We would be in the hospital inside of a day – well I would, Chris is made of sterner stuff.

We've never travelled or had a gap year like a lot of my friends in their younger years. *(I'm obviously going to get into trouble for this comment, as it suggests they are now old!)* They embarked on the backpacking, travelling adventures in their teens/early twenties. For various reasons we never did this, mainly because I hate camping, or roughing it. I mean really hate it. I get told off for saying this word, but I'm just very passionate about things. I might hate some stuff, but I LOVE other things – like Cappuccinos and Porn Star Martinis... so it all balances out in the end.

On the holiday front, I never went abroad as a kid. We'd go away as a big gang with other families to Butlins, so holidays abroad were not something I ever aspired to. I also never thought about the wide world that much. So, going to Faliraki in Greece with my housemate for my first foreign holiday was a bit of an eye opener. During this holiday I met my Other Half. After a holiday romance, fast forward twenty years and here we are.

I digress – back to day one...

At 11.30am we are collected by Chris's parents who are kindly taking us to the train station. Sitting on the station it all seems surreal, this adventure we've been discussing and planning for two years, talking to our friends and family about and in all likelihood boring them to death. The day is finally here. It's been a rocky road in some ways. We both applied for unpaid leave, which was granted and then shortly after they offered redundancies at my place of work. At this point in my life, I'd started writing a book in April 2018, and finished it all bar the editing in a month. At 43 years of age I'd started my writing career, I won't bore you with all the details. If you care to check out my website it will tell you all about it... www.clpeache.com.

Anyway, I decided to take redundancy and spent the 7 months before this epic journey writing and networking.

Back to day one... sorry got distracted by life again... I do that...

The train arrives on time – which will be a theme for the holiday. It seems we're fortunate that way. Even a delay in Sydney results in me watching a film whilst drinking wine. I will take that for a delay any day of the week.

On the train, I have to ask a woman to move from our pre-booked seats, but she moves without putting up a fight, with maybe just a hint of irritation. We settle into our journey to London. I cannot help but earwig on a conversation the woman is having with what I deduce is her soon-to-be or already ex-partner. I will never know why people have such personal conversations in public places, but hey, what can you do but listen? Be careful people, a writer might just be listening…

After a smooth and comfortable journey, we arrive at Kings Cross and drag ourselves, the cases and the heavy rucksacks across to St Pancras where we navigate a lot of pissed off looking people and head to the pub. We find a spot and order drinks and food. The table service does make life easier, especially when we have loads of luggage. During the wait, we reflect that we cannot believe we are here. This is the start of our dream holiday. What will happen? Who will we meet? Will it all go as planned?

I, of course, spend the time checking we have our passports, documents and continually wondering what our first long haul flight will be like. The feeling of disbelief that the time has come is still lingering. We are firm believers that you gain as much pleasure from looking forward to a holiday as doing it. Spending weeks, months, years knowing you have a holiday in the diary, really helps those long days at work and the dreary dark nights.

After killing a few hours, we head back to Kings Cross to catch the train to Heathrow. It takes 45 minutes; this is 45 minutes spent trying not to look at anyone on the underground. I've visited London many times and feel I have perfected the thousand-yard stare. It can be challenging to master – if you don't get it just right you look mad or if you do make eye contact, it's all very awkward. A group of musicians get on and treat us to 5 minutes of music before offering their caps up for some cash. Good on them, it brightens up a boring journey. I think the advertising companies are missing a trick by not plastering the tube floors; you have a captive audience right there desperate for something to look at.

Arriving at Heathrow, we make our way to check-in. We have been lucky enough to fly many times before, but this is our first long haul flight. We decide to brave the self-service check-in points as we're grown-ups, sophisticated and tech-savvy; obviously, my passport doesn't scan. *(Insert rolled eyes.)*

We stand in line. Is it just us or do some people take like a gazillion years to do anything? Honestly, there is epic faffing going on, bags on, bags off the check-in weigh scales, cases opened and closed. Surely you weighed your bags before you left? Or people take coats out. Why, oh why, wait until check-in, you idiots!

Wait for it, wait for it, someone then moves one of the sectioned off security barriers for the queue, which by the way no-one seems to acknowledge in the terminal. *(I'm not quite sure why they have them.)* Then we have, wait for it... the queue stand off! One of the best and most exciting things to behold for a Brit. A man and a woman are at the front of the queue, next in line. The pusher-in is hanging about in front, get this – in front of the couple first in the queue. Looking around, all the Brits in the queue are waiting with bated breath at this development. No other nationality seems even to notice. The couple shuffles forward a few steps and turn their bodies – a clear Brit indication that they have your number and no way in hell are you getting past. The Brits' anxiety levels are through the roof. We despise queue jumpers, it infuriates us, the audacity! The Brit might even have to say something, actually articulate their displeasure in words. The queuing Brits inwardly gasp, eyes wide with excitement. This makes the delay to checking-in completely worth it.

Finally, the two people at the check-in desk move on, and the queuing couple head to the counter at lightning speed, only to be turned away as the official has decided she's taking someone from another queue. Gutted. They shuffle back, hoping that another Brit will recognise that by the rules of queuing they should be allowed to remain at the front. They do.

In the meantime, the pusher-in has made his move further forward. You can almost slice the tension with a boarding card. *(If we had one.)* What is going to happen? The couple by this time are back, and position themselves in front of the pusher-in. Finally, the pair faffing with their overweight bags sort themselves out, and the check-in desk is free again. The Brits' bodies are leaning forward, all thoughts of holiday nerves forgotten. The pusher-in makes his move, but the couple sprint forward faster than my hand reaching out for a free drink on the plane. The checker-in gets three passports waved in her face. She does not look happy, which is pretty much 'the look' in all the airports I've flown from in the UK. It seems their main aim is to be grumpy. Although, we discover that this is only the UK airports; in every other airport the staff manage to smile, be friendly and still do a professional job. Sorry to any of the nice ones in the UK – maybe we just haven't crossed paths.

Back to the desk…

The pusher-in tries to explain something to the couple, but they have closed their ears and minds. They were first. End of. The checker-in has to explain to the couple that she asked the pusher-in to come back. Oooohhhhhh dear, this has not gone well for the couple; they have been defeated; everything they ever surmised about queues has been dashed, they might as well go home now. Holiday ruined. They stuck to their queue rights, and they lost. Heads down they try to return to the queue, but everyone else has moved forward to the red line to make sure they got a good look at the drama, so they have to stand in shame beyond the red line; something utterly alien to a Brit. The queuers' sigh. We live for scenes like this. This tale will reach far and wide – well I've put it in this travel journal, that's how important it is. What a great start to our holiday. Predictably we check-in and it goes smoothly, and we are bagless in approximately 5 minutes. Again, we comment on why it takes others so long.

We get through security with no problems and hang about in the terminal until it's time to board. Again, all goes smoothly, and before long we're on the plane. Predictably people are faffing taking stuff out of their bags, holding up the whole of the flight. Why do people not do this before? Why? Finally, we are seated, and I bag the window seat – result! Chris had bagged it, but because of people messing about the air stewardess came over to sort them out and she gestured for me to take a seat after she had shifted them. What could I do? Winner.

It's a novelty having a screen and films available to watch on the flight, you don't get these on short haul flights that I've been on. The trip goes smoothly, other than trying to get to sleep. Even though these planes have more room I still cannot get comfy. I did contemplate trying to sneak into business class – I've got my laptop with me after all, but I decide it's not worth it.

We enjoy two meals on the plane – well I say enjoy; they are not bad for plane food. We find out we get free alcohol! Again, as a Brit, I love free stuff, especially free alcohol. Plus, I muse on the flight, if we crash landed like in the series Lost – at least I could enjoy a glass of wine while waiting to be rescued. We arrive at Changi airport in Singapore a little earlier than planned, and surprisingly, the nearly 13-hour flight has been okay. Before this, we'd only logged 4.5 hours as a maximum flight time, and this doesn't seem that much different.

Whilst I have the luxury of editing this at home, I'm able to look up these fascinating areas we have travelled over. I look at the photos I'd taken out of the window. Even though phones are not supposed to work in airplane mode, the photos have the location on. During the flight we flew over Ahal; Turkmenistan in Central Asia, which borders the Caspian Sea and Afghanistan on the mainland. Riau Island; Province of Indonesia. Amazing that life is happening right below us, whilst we are flying halfway around the world.

Day one of the holiday is over, and we are ready for the sights and sounds of Singapore. I'm not sure we are ready for the humidity though...

Total Spent: £33.40

Total spends for the day will be included at the end of the chapter as well as where we stayed, what the accommodation was like, area, tourist sites we visited and how much everything cost. There will be a break down the cost of everything at the end of the book. If you want to see how much fuel we used, the price of a Crunchie – this is the one book where you can flick to the end without ruining the ending. I will probably rant a bit, and be opinionated, but you have read this far – you might as well carry on.

Singapore

Day 2 | Tuesday 19th February

We only have one full day in Singapore, so our plans are not to make too many plans. We weren't sure if we would suffer any jetlag, and Singapore is a stop off place for our main trip to New Zealand. Our idea is to make sure we're ready for that. If that means sleeping, then so be it. But, we are mindful that it's not every day you get to experience these countries.

We left on Monday 18th at 8.25pm and arrive after a 13 hours flight on Tuesday 19th at 5.30pm. We try desperately not to work out the time at home. We fail, of course. Singapore is eight hours ahead of the UK, and it feels slightly weird.

The security goes without a hitch, and I finally have a stamp in my passport. This is a momentous occasion, but the security bloke doesn't seem to care. We have to put our thumbs on a tablet to secure our passage into Singapore. I wonder what they are going to do with that data? If you don't provide it, you're not getting into the country, so there's not much choice on the matter.

Bags collected, we get changed into our holiday gear in preparation for the Singapore heat. We pre packed a bag which had loose fitting clothes in so we were ready for the heat, and I can recommend that you do this; in fact, this could be my first TOP TIP. We head to the terminal area to catch a cab to our hotel, which is well worth the money. The first thing that strikes us is how like England it is… apart from the humidity of course, which feels like someone is following you around with a hairdryer on full blast.

Singapore was a colonial country. If you are travelling here, I recommend reading up on the country and watching some YouTube videos.

The history is fascinating, and you understand where the British influence comes from. Raffles certainly made his impression on Singapore.

It feels bizarre to head around the world only to feel like you're in the UK, apart from the heat as I've said. Singapore is HOT, hot and humid and takes some adjusting to. It also changes our plans due to me being unable to cope with this kind of heat. *(Yes, I know, once again typical Brits. Moan about the cold, moan about the heat….)* We could push through and turn up at our hotel like drowned sweaty rats, but this trip is not about hardship.

Arriving at the hotel, the Furama Riverside, the porter takes our bags, and we head to the reception area. The lovely lady checks us in, and we confirm the 4pm late check out we requested as part of our club executive bedroom. It comes with access to the club lounge room which includes free cocktails between 6–8pm; although we discovered it's not cocktails, it's free drinks. I opt for a rum and coke, but I think they forgot the coke. *The next night I ask for a rum and pineapple with only a little rum – this was perfect.* This also comes with free nibbles which is like having a tapas meal. So, the room is a little more expensive than others we have seen, but the benefits certainly make up for it. Travel books and friends have told us that Singapore is expensive, and it is, but only as much as a capital city such as London, and only if you opt to eat and drink out all the time. The food halls of the Hawker centres are the place to go to experience the sights and smells of Singapore and the food is cheap – they are an experience not to be missed.

The room is fancy, the bed could fit approximately 4.5 people in it, the waterfall shower has a rough pumice slate which provides welcome relief on hot, sweaty feet. They also have a retractable clothesline in the bathroom which is handy for our swimming things.

After dumping our cases in the hotel room, and taking a refreshing shower, we make our way to the club room for the last 40 minutes of free drinks. I mean why would you miss out when you've paid for it? The staff here are so nice, they make you feel very welcome, and the service is fantastic. They have a selection of food which is welcome after a long flight. Generally, we're very chilled about travelling, but we also feel the anxiety of a long flight, wondering what it is going to be like, had we booked the right places? How will we deal with any problems?

The food and drink wakes us up, and we decide to brave the heat of Singapore on our first night. The hotel doors open and the wall of heat hits us, although after a few minutes we accept that sweatiness will be our constant companion when not in an air conditioned building. We've checked the maps and head in the rough direction of China Town.

We are so glad we took the decision to go out. It would have been easy to stay inside and let jetlag dictate the evening. Walking to China town, we take in the sights and sounds of the streets of Singapore. It's an interesting contrast. Singapore feels very English obviously, all the signs are in English, but the people are very different.

The smells from the Hawker centres are overpowering, and my stomach rumbles even though I'm not hungry.

Every shaded area, under every building has a person sheltering from the heat and humidity, which is approximately 28 degrees at 8.30pm. *(On our journey home a wonderful taxi driver tells us that Singapore has a wide weather band of between 26–34 degrees.)*

China Town is well worth a visit, just immerse yourself in the experience. As we are walking around, we come across a Chinese Dragon display by the Sim San Loke Hup Lantern

Festival; big crowds gather to watch the show. Mobile phones raised high to capture the event. Experiences like this are what holidays are all about.

Having the luxury of time now I do some research into the festival. They visited various businesses where they put fruit on the floor in offering to the dragons, who then performed the dance to bring them good luck. Well worth a look online at the videos.

After drinking loads of water, we inevitably find ourselves desperate for the toilet. This doesn't prove easy at this time of night. We head into a shopping centre that looks shut, and a security guard recognises us as new tourists and asks if he can help. This is Singapore, people are friendly and are happy to help, rather than it just being their job to do so.

After a bit more wandering, I can highly recommend this in Singapore. Just wander and take in the sights and smells, try to stay away from the packed tourist areas and look at where the locals are eating and drinking. We head back to the hotel, satisfied and tired. A fabulous start to our trip. Already we feel like we've done a lot, and we've only been in the country a few hours. We gratefully go back to our air conditioned room, with some water and a bottle of beer for Chris.

Accommodation: Furama Riverside
Nights: 2
Number: 1736
Type: Club executive room
Facilities: None
Price: £214.96
Wifi: Free – important to keep roaming costs to a minimum
CheckIn: Fast and smooth
Parking: N/A
Weather: 32 degrees, hot and humid
Skin Colour: Pale as pastry from the English winter
Bites: None – but this number will sadly increase!

Total Spent: $32.20 / £18*

The conversion rates are based on the rates when we travelled and rounded up to the nearest pound. Further information at the back for the spreadsheet geeks like me.

Singapore
Day 3 | Wednesday 20th February

We wake feeling okay, the jet lag doesn't seem to be doing too much damage. We make our way to the breakfast room, where there isn't exactly a vast choice for a vegetarian, and Chris settles for toast and pastries, while I indulge in some crispy streaky bacon and a poached egg on cheesy tomatoes. The absolute bonus – free and good cappuccinos. As a coffee addict this is more than welcome. It also means we don't have to rush out to find a coffee shop to satisfy my need for decent coffee. *(We've had to do this on many holidays.)*

After breakfast, we decide to make use of the large swimming pool outside. It's bliss to sink into the pool although Chris still has to drag me in. I'm a wuss when it comes to getting into a pool. I'm sure my screams can be heard across the city. Once in though, it's wonderful. There is nothing like lounging in a pool to make you feel like you're on holiday. We hang about until some kids decide they want to come and scream and play right next to us, despite having a massive pool at their disposal. The parents have somehow used their magical powers to deduce I used to look after children as my profession, and mentally, without permission, sign over the adoption paper to us. We head out, content with the quiet time we've managed and ready to see the sights of Singapore.

After walking for five minutes, we immediately realise that we're not going to manage more than fifteen minutes before we need to lie in a freezer to recover. Think The Snowman. We do the sensible thing and decide to explore the delights of the city using the hop on/hop off bus. This is the best decision yet.

As with all these buses you get the audio guide and we spend a pleasant day taking in the delights of the red and yellow lines, sometimes braving the heat of upstairs, which does allow a breeze. But, there is also the absolute heaven of the air-conditioned downstairs. Really, is there a better feeling than getting out of the sweaty, clammy, pumping heat and your body being enveloped by the cooling air conditioning?

The blue line takes us around every road that seems to be named after Raffles. I suppose since he planted the flag and decided the UK was claiming the country, it's not so surprising. The Raffles Hotel is the place where the famous Singapore Sling cocktail was invented. Unfortunately, it's closed for refurbishment, and in the end, I enjoy a free Singapore Sling on the plane to Auckland. I cannot help it if I'm tight and the bar is closed! I'm from Yorkshire after all. We pass stunning parks and huge buildings; one turns out to be a hospital for the rich who come and try to look younger and change what nature gave them. I'm not judgemental; just jealous that I cannot afford it. Although looking at some of the rich and famous, I think it's best to stay clear of surgery. The bus takes us through Little India and back around the loop, before dropping us at the bus terminal so we can change routes.

The bus terminal has a shopping centre where you can make use of the air-conditioning; it has loads of shops as well as toilets, food and drinks. Which is very useful while you're waiting for your next bus. You can catch all the various routes from here, and the guides are friendly and informative.

The red line takes in the fantastic sight of Marina Bay Sands Hotel. Wow, I'm sure you have to flash a different coloured Visa card to the receptionist than I possess.

We travel across the Helix Bridge, around the Singapore Flyer. *(Version of the London Eye.)* We see the area they use for F1 pit stops. We used to be fans of F1, but got bored; basically, because the races were won in the pits or decided by officials after the race. Now we only watch Motorbike racing because they actually race. Not that you really needed to know all of that. We go past the Marina Bay Sands Hotel again and then head around the China Town area we visited last night. We decide to alight and head back to the hotel to freshen up and make use of the free food and drinks. This really did save us a lot of money, so the trade-off for the more expensive hotel was financially the right call.

We make use of the pool as we can see it from the window of our hotel; we check that no parents are hanging around waiting for some potential victims to look after their kids. *(Not all parents are like this I might add.)* After a dip in the pool we return to the lounge for nibbles and drinks before we brave the humidity for a walk along the Singapore River to the Quayside. This is well worth the stroll; it's a stunning, vibrant place with wonderful smells and live bands; it's a welcome assault on the senses and an exciting place to be. We sniff out a real ale pub, and partake of a drink or two.

In the hotel we reflect on an enjoyable visit around Singapore. I think if you want comfort and ease then the buses are the way to go. They take all the work out of it, but you're still seeing the sights.

Total Spent: *$142.95/£80*

Singapore to Auckland

Day 4 or 5 | Thursday 21st & Friday 22nd February *have no idea*

Day Four follows the same format as yesterday. After a swim we head out to catch the bus, as the pass is valid for 24 hours from time of purchase. We wander into China Town to get the bus, but decide to head into the shopping centre to cool down. Okay, I'm going to admit that we went into a McDonalds for lunch. There I said it. Judge as you see fit; we should have gone local, should have immersed ourselves in the experience. But, plenty of locals were eating there so it was fair game, and it was air-conditioned!

After this we catch the bus from Speakers' Corner. We find out on our return journey that we could have caught the bus across the road from our hotel but never mind. Basically, apart from getting off to swap buses and have lunch we spend many enjoyable hours on the bus again. We do the yellow line which takes you past Marina Sands Hotel; of course, it does. We travel over the river to the Botanical Gardens, past lots of fancy buildings on Orchard Road which seems to go on forever. Then it is back to the bus terminal to hop on the brown route which takes us along Havelock Road and near the Clarke Quay area we enjoyed last night. It skirts China Town again and the National Gallery. We get off for a coffee stop before heading to the terminal to catch the red bus again. This time we go on the full loop around Little India, taking in the impressive National Museum of Singapore and lots of other sights. Grateful again for the air conditioning, we part company with our buses; they really have been a lifeline and made Singapore so much more enjoyable. We have to catch our flight this evening, so we return to the hotel.

Check-out is predictably smooth, efficient and friendly. We have a few hours to kill before we need to head to the airport, so we make use of the hotel lounge bar. Be warned… the cakes are massive and delicious. We find a quiet area, and to the backdrop of a waterfall in the hotel gardens, I sit typing up some of this journal. After a while, the Other Half gets twitchy. So, I order us some cake, beer for him and a glass of soft stuff for myself. It's an actual holiday highlight for Chris as when he's finished his beer, the all-seeing and all-knowing waiter brings over another fresh and frothy glass of beer and announces its buy one get one free. Chris thinks he's died and gone to beer holiday heaven.

***

It's a pleasure to enter Changi Airport, it must be one of the best airports in the world for service and facilities and by the sound of it there is lots more to come. It was worth the $24 dollars for the taxi from the hotel to departures. The thought of tackling the metro or the bus in 34-degree heat is unthinkable. Not when we've budgeted enough, and have spent very little on our days out. It's a luxury we can afford.

In Changi airport we check our departure gate and find one of the check-in machines. Usually my passport doesn't work, I don't know what the UK systems have against it, but everywhere else it is fine. Checked in and bag tags added, I cannot help but wonder if this is really making life better. Yes, maybe it's a bit quicker, but where is the holiday interaction? As social media blooms, are we becoming more anti-social? More comfortable with a screen on a machine telling us what to do? Where to go? I cannot help but feel like we are missing out on those random few minutes' chats, where you pass the time of day and put the world to rights. Or in the case of the UK; the grunts. Maybe that's just my age and my crisis to deal with.

Bags weighed and put into the care of the airport by another machine, we make our way to security, thinking we would be headed into the hustle of the usual airport. Oh no, they have a Butterfly House; they screen free films for your comfort; not to mention the fabulous places to dine on the second floor. Wow. It's worth flying here just to visit the airport.

We've booked a seat upstairs on the plane, because let's face it, who goes on a double decker plane and doesn't book a seat upstairs? Oh, and they had two seats together rather than the usual three at the side, which was really nice for that romantic couple on holiday.

The flight is smooth as usual, many films are watched, many drinks are drunk – including the Singapore Sling I mentioned earlier. Singapore Airlines are very attentive and customer focused. Nothing is too much trouble. Not that we need much looking after other than our food and the odd drink. Not like some folk. Honestly, I think they live to be awkward. I don't know how the staff remain smiling. Good job I didn't take up that profession – although I would need a step ladder to reach the overhead luggage.

Right, that's Singapore done and dusted and onto New Zealand to start our road trip – so excited!

Total Spent: *$94.40/£53*

Part Two: The North

Auckland

Day 5 | Friday 22nd February

We catch the bus from the airport, and have already gone against our rule of getting taxis and making life easy. It proves to be a good move though, as I sit next to someone who will happily chat with anyone – just like me, and we spend the time-sharing stories on a packed bus. She's returned to visit New Zealand after a long time away and is reminiscing about old times. We discover we have a shared love of skydiving, myself being the amateur as I've only managed one. She tells me the best place to jump out of a plane is Wanaka, and spending a day there later in our travels, I can see why. The lake is sublimely beautiful, and I can imagine how stunning a skydive would be; more about that later. By the end of the conversation we decide we are going to open a skydiving school; mainly so we can skydive for free.

    She talks about how religious they are in New Zealand, which is something I've never really thought about or heard about really. I come to believe her after seeing the number of TV channels devoted to religion. It seems a weird combination to have a mixture of faith with a relaxed attitude towards guns. We come to discover it is a way of life here. I'm not judging that it is wrong; although at the moment, we,

I, this country and the world, is blissfully unaware that someone is planning to attack this beautiful island and change the people that live here forever, and quite frankly it will change how the world sees this country and it's gun laws. That said, New Zealand is a beautiful, friendly place, which deserves a special place in your heart.

We get off the bus on Queens Street, which is the main shopping road in Auckland and survey the place we have checked out on the internet. It's pretty much the same as any high street in the UK.

After consulting Chris's phone for directions, we head up Shortland Street and follow the road around onto Eden Crescent. At this point I should mention there are a couple of hills, my screaming calves and back are testament to this, typically only being used to the flat lands of Lincolnshire and Newark which don't have many hills to boast about – thankfully. The hill is not the best sight when you're carrying two heavy rucksacks, two cases and a laptop bag, but sometimes it's going be hard, even though we have tried to make this trip as duffer-friendly as possible. We are not spring chickens, so this will not be a trip of backpacking, suffering and mucking in – oh no, I'm knocking on the door of my mid-forties, *(Excuse me while I just digest that and freak out…)* while Chris is 50 this year *(Suddenly I don't feel so bad!)*

We make it to the apartment and receive a lovely welcome and a speedy check-in. The woman is very friendly and politely doesn't mention our jet-lagged, sweaty faces. She does, however, mention that our apartment has the best views. Exactly what you want to hear after a 10-hour flight, a bus ride and a sweaty walk. The lift takes us to our apartment, the doors open onto a beautiful hallway, and I've mentally moved in.

Wow, she wasn't kidding, the view of the harbour and city is amazing. We can see the dock area going about its day. I love watching the day to day life of a place. Much later in the year when we are watching Henry Cole's Motorcycle rides again, he stays in a very similar area. We freeze frame to see if it's the same apartment; but alas it isn't. It always seems such a thrill to see somewhere you've been on TV. The apartment is better than we expected. Well equipped, with a washer and dryer; which is very useful.

We could probably both do with a wash and tumble dry. It has a large comfy bed. I would 100% recommend staying here – especially if you can get this room.

So, I'm sitting here in our fabulous apartment appreciating life…

Sometime later…

I had to stop writing as we went to the local supermarket, about an 8–10 minute walk from the apartment to pick up essentials like an Indian microwave meal, *(Living the dream.)* booze, *(Obvs.)* and other essentials like coffee, tea, butter and bagels – I won't give you the whole list, some of the food we purchased is at the back of this book; you don't have to read all that of course, but I like assimilating this information; if you don't, then feel free not to read it to the end. I bet you're one of those people who doesn't sit to the end of the credits at the cinema just in case something happens.

It's started raining, and the cool breeze is welcome after the humidity of Singapore. After a long flight and travelling, we are suitably knackered and decide to call it an early night and prepare ourselves for our only full day in Auckland.

How strange it feels to be here after all the planning.

Accommodation: Quest on Eden Apartments
Nights: 2
Number: 8G *(Get this apartment if you can.)*
Type: Apartment
Facilities: Well equipped. Hob, sink, washing machine/dryer
Price: £176.64
Wi-fi: Free *(Although they had limited data at 512MB which didn't seem to last long, even though I was using WhatsApp/Facebook/messenger.)*
Check-In: Fast, friendly and smooth
Parking: N/A

Weather: Slightly Sweaty; humid, started cloudy, then came the welcome rain after the heat of Singapore

Skin Colour: Still pale as pastry from the English winter, although red from being sweaty.

Bites: None

Total Spent: *$106.38/£55*

Auckland

Day 6 | Saturday 23rd February

Our first morning waking up in Auckland, and I've woken feeling refreshed from the flight/time difference coma I slipped into. I felt exhausted at about 8pm last night and couldn't fight it – jet lag for you. After arriving at our apartment yesterday, I managed to get a full sweaty Singapore batch of washing done, folded and put away, and guess what? There is… a sock missing! How can this happen? In an apartment we have been in less than 24 hours? There were two, and now there is only one. So, I won't be leaving my heart in New Zealand; it will just be my sock. Well, Chris's sock to be precise.

It's 7am and it still feels weird that it's Friday night in the UK. I spend some time catching up with friends back home, assuring mum that I'm safe and have not been kidnapped by pirates. *(What a story that would be.)* After that, it's writing up my journal and updating this very book you're reading. Some readers are no doubt screaming at the page or surprised we're not out making the most of the day – what's that saying, 'Seize the day?' Well, it's our day and we will seize, or not, at our leisure.

We are doing this trip our way. As I've mentioned we're not spring chickens who can run around all day, bungee jumping, boat rafting, walking around the city – we're too old for all that. *Well, actually we're not too old, on return from this holiday we took up kayaking, so I guess we still have life left in us yet.* We just choose to do things in a more luxurious and chilled out pace so we don't physically pay for it later. Slowly does it. If you spend your life rushing about, how much of that time are you spending looking up and taking it in? So, you might be able to tell people confidently you went to all the 'tourist' destinations?

Each to their own, if that's what floats your boat. My aim for this trip was to feel like I live here, day one and I can already say that its mission accomplished. Chris is playing his game, I'm writing, we both have cappuccinos next to the bed. It's a time to sit and appreciate life and where we are.

As I type, the mist and forecast rain is heading over the headland. From our apartment we have a great view of the wharves. Marsden Wharf, Captain Cook Wharf and Queens Wharf. I've already watched a massive cruise ship arrive at the passenger terminal; these all sit in Waitemata Harbour. Although I'm reminded of James Herbert's *'The Fog'*; as the mist is starting to encompass the large cargo cranes threatening zero visibility to the dock workers. Our view of the islands is already obscured from the comfort of my bed.

Another interruption to this journal… just had to take a comfort break… yes, I know this might be too much information, but all this travelling, eating rich food, drinking every day – having free alcohol included in our room rate in Singapore might not have been the best idea on reflection. But, anyway, this travel journal keeps it real, and being regular is essential. If I don't maintain my regular bowel movements, I will run out of indigestion remedies *(I wonder if someone will sponsor this if I give them a shout out.)* and if my bloatedness gets anymore out of hand they will be selling tickets to visit the first-ever living, breathing, landlocked whale! Right that's that out of the way; see we are going to know each other really well now. After a lovely morning we are off to get ready and explore the delights of Auckland. More later…

Much later...

Weather: Changeable condition/light rain showers most of the day.

We spend a fab afternoon wandering around Auckland and taking in the sights and sounds. Exactly like being in any UK city or large town. Some parts remind us of Scarborough with the tree-lined streets and the hills sloping down to the sea. We find the nearest Spark shop first, which is their version of O2/Vodaphone to get our sims cards organised for our road trip around New Zealand. These cost $29 each for 1GB data and 200 Min calls/ 200 texts. You can also top these up easily enough once you've registered. We make our way to a pretty arcade towards the sea end of Queens Street and find a nice coffee shop upstairs in the arcade, called Coffee Club. Excellent service and a lovely balcony where we chill out and sort out our phones. Two coffees are $9.

Coffee finished I decide I need the loo. No, before you think it, I'm not going to go on about my toilet habits throughout the whole journal, I do have a reason for this. So, imagine a beautiful shopping arcade which looks very posh, clean, with boutique style shops, tiled shiny walls. So, I think I will make use of the toilets. I go inside and on other days I'm sure they are as lovely as the arcade, but unfortunately today the smell is horrific and not just what you think. A girl comes out of one of the toilets, I go in and come straight back out again.

She says, "Horrible innit?"

I reply, "Yes, not very nice at all."

She says, "Nope, not very nice at all." As she washes her filthy hands which look like she's recently used them to smear something. I will leave it to your imagination to picture what is smeared all over the toilet seat and walls. The other main smell is emanating from the girl. I would say she is in her early twenties, with a lot of teeth missing and the rest of her is not in a good state.

I feel very sorry for her. This is not to judge Auckland or New Zealand in any way, every city around the world sadly has people who live like this. She was pleasant enough to me,

I just feel sad that people have to live and behave that way. I might have said earlier this journal would be a reflection of real life; warts and all.

I think it's encounters like this that make you realise life is still going on around you. While we are in the 'holiday' bubble, enjoying life, other people are living with their day-to-day problems. It's true to say some people have really shit lives. Sometimes self-inflicted and sometimes not. I suppose that's why it's so important to grab every experience in life. We are after all 'only here once' unless you believe in reincarnation of course, but that's for another book, probably not written by me.

Leaving the arcade, we head towards the sea, just as the fine rain starts. *(It's spitting, everybody in – if you're not a Peter Kay fan you won't get that – sorry.)* We make it to the harbour and spend a lovely time taking in the sights of the massive cruise ships and boats that are docked. We head for a bar called Crab Shack and immediately feel like we've been transported to the '90s, *'I think we're alone now'* by Tiffany and many other similar songs welcoming the disembarking passengers. A beer and a fizz help us to chill out and take in the vibe of the area. We watch tourists coming and going, making up our own little stories about them, where they come from, the lives they have back home.

Auckland is a cool city with a lot to offer, it's a shame we only have one day to explore this lovely place. I will say that after only one day, we tune into its vibe and thoroughly enjoy it. Following our drinks, we go on to explore the harbour area. We intended to go up the Sky Tower, but the weather isn't in our favour, so we decide against it. Maybe another day or another time will present itself, and it's a reason to come back if nothing else.

In the evening when we head to the supermarket to get our food for dinner and some breakfast items, we make the usual tourist mistake and get lost. I blame the jet lag rather than Chris and his map reading skills – or map on his phone should I add. I can't be bothered to argue that I told him we were going the wrong way.

En route we've visited Albert Park; this is well worth a visit. The trees are amazing, and it's got a chilled-out vibe going on, as much of Auckland does. If you like weird shaped trees, tall trees, plum trees, any kind of trees, then you need to visit this park. It also has some fantastic views of Auckland and the Sky Tower.

Right, that's the end of day one in Auckland and day six of our travels. Tomorrow we collect the car from the airport and move on to Pukenui, which is approximately five hours from Auckland. We will be headed towards the North where we intend to visit beaches and Cape Reinga, which is the furthest North you can go on the island.

We're looking forward to picking up the car and starting our road trip of New Zealand.

Total Spent: *$174.05/£91*

Pukenui

Day 7 | Sunday 24th February

The day starts off very relaxed despite neither of us sleeping that well, thinking about the day ahead. It's time to pick up the car and start the road trip of a lifetime. I make us a drink in bed before starting to organise our bags. When you're away for so long it pays to take a bit of time to sort out your possessions, especially when Chris isn't exactly organised. When I packed for the flights, I'd split our clothing into each case, a good idea in case one bag goes missing – at least you both have some clothes. I'd sorted them so that we each had our own case of clothes. It would save him rummaging through mine and creasing them all.

But, I've organised them a day too early as we don't have the car to leave our cases in yet, so I went with shoving stuff where it would fit. Anyway, no bother. Chris went on an app and ordered us a cab to take us to the car hire place as it's outside Auckland airport. The bus would have cost $38, the taxi was a fixed price at $35 and picked us up from our apartment and dropped us at the car hire place.

About forty-five minutes before the taxi is due, Chris says, "Have we got any cash for the cab?"

I reply, "I hope so. I mentioned it at least a hundred billion times yesterday not to spend all the cash and use the cards."

Turns out he's spent the last of the cash. *(Insert rolling eyes.)* I bite my tongue nearly in half trying not to say, "I told you not to."

He wisely decides to go and find a cash point whilst I carry on tidying the apartment and finish the packing.

Chris arrives back just in time after a frantic search for a cash machine. I chew at the other half of my tongue trying not to say it's your own fault. Bless him, I feel bad as he is actually a bit stressed about it. We check out and get in the cab. On the journey we reflect that we really needed more time in Auckland. We hadn't had time to do anything, but we knew time would be against us on this trip and New Zealand was more about the road trip for us. I would love to come back here and do more activities one day. I leave Auckland feeling like we tuned into the heart of the city, and that, for me, makes memories.

As usual we have problems at the car hire place when they try to charge us extra for insurance even though Chris made sure that we were covered. Luckily, we're over-organised and prepared for this. I don't want to talk ill of car hire companies, but we have been stung before for extra payments that were not warranted. After a look at the paperwork and a phone call, it is agreed that we are right.

> **TOP TIP:** *Make sure you print every single document and read the small print!*

After a bit of a stressful morning, holidays are not always perfect. Luckily, we have learnt to let things go. "I told you so," or "It's your fault," are not helpful and just cause a bad atmosphere. I tend to WhatsApp my friends and rant. That way, I get the frustration out of my system without us falling out. Darn it, Chris will find out my secret ranting messages now… might have to tell him to skip this chapter! Surely all partners know we text our best mates everything? *(They do now… Sorry.)*

Finally, the car hire is sorted, and we pack the car for the first time. Our red Suzuki Swift will do us proud over our road trip. At the end of our journey, it's a shame to let it go.

A car becomes another companion on a trip. If we ever go back to NZ, it would be good to have the same vehicle.

We stop off at McDonald's – I know, I know. As I have said, I'm addicted to coffee, and we need one. Also, we set up the toll account while in the car park so that we don't get any further charges along the way. It's easy to set up as long as you have the internet, so make sure you have your sim card sorted by this point. Toll set up and paid for, coffee in our claws, we set off. Chris has to get used to driving an automatic, so he takes it easy for about five minutes and then he's off, since he has the ability to drive just about anything. I don't drive so cannot share the load, which suits us both. I was born to be driven and Chris likes driving; so, it's win win.

Our first stop before we take to the road in earnest is to head to the department store to purchase some cool bags. We can then transport our food and butties each day. As we are staying in self-catering apartments and want to spend as little as possible on food. The cool bags come in handy later when we arrive at our accommodation and slip our fizz and beer into it and make our way to the edge of Pukenui Bay.

The drive over the bridge as we head out of Auckland is stunning, and sets the scene for the rest of the journey. If I were to compare it to other places, this drive is like a little bit of the Lake District, Yorkshire Dales, Scotland, Cornwall, Ireland with a sub-tropical theme running through the middle. The views are breath-taking; the photos really don't do it justice. I still manage to take about fifty – God knows how I'm going to sort them out when I get home.

On this subject, we are now at the point where we are downloading all our photos to try to get them in order. We took some using our phones and some with the camera. Last count was 4,000! It's a mammoth task. These are now available on my website. Luckily for you there is only a small selection.

Not long out of Auckland we stop at the services to eat the sandwiches we made back in apartment 8G. Does anyone else want to eat their butties as soon as they set off? Anyway, it's about 11am and it's been a long old morning, so we find a services to pull over and take in this epic journey we've started. It's like going back to services in UK in the '80s. A few times we've said we cannot believe we are here. I think because it seems so familiar it's hard to take in that we are on the other side of the world.

The views are stunning; if you're thinking of doing a trip like this, just do it. Do whatever you can to make it happen. Sell your soul, your Grandma… literally anything. You will not be disappointed. It seems around every corner and over every hill, there is a different vista for your eyes to gorge on. We've said 'wow' repeatedly and this is our first day on the road. So, it bodes well for the rest of the journey. After a while, you guessed it – we stop for a coffee. It's quite interesting because as we are waiting for our coffees, a local bloke is hanging about, and naturally he gravitates towards Chris. First, he shows him how to fold his ear over to entertain his grandkids, then he asks if Chris has any grandkids; to which he answers no. *(I'm sniggering in the corner, avoiding eye contact.)* The bloke asks for a bag of coffee grinds from the girl behind the counter, and proceeds to tell Chris that they are good for the garden and they keep the white butterflies away, or so he'd heard on the radio yesterday. I find this all highly entertaining to listen to.

Our journey from Auckland to Pukenui takes us through Westhaven, the Dairy Flat, Puhoi, Pohuehue, Warkworth, Wellsford, Topuni, Kaiwaka, Waipu, Hikurangi, Paihia, Kokopu, Kaeo, Totara North, Mangonui, Taipa, before finally arriving at our destination, Pukenui. I know all of these, not because of my incredible geographical knowledge, or map reading skills, *(Non-existent.)* but, because I took so many photos and the iPhone kindly adds the locations for me. Thank you, Apple.

During our drive through these places we've experienced sunny rain showers, and stunning scenery to arrive finally at our home for the next few days. Breath-taking views will be our constant companion throughout this trip.

Pukenui Lodge Motel sits next to the Rangaunu Bay, which is stunningly beautiful, the light reflecting off the water is magical. Boats bob about on the bay and birds dive bomb the water trying to catch their next meal. After checking into the hotel and unpacking, we make our way across the road to the supermarket, which closes at 7pm.

Stir-fry dinner made, we head to the water to enjoy a drink and reflect on another fantastic day in New Zealand – this place is delivering the goods.

I simply cannot do the views justice as we sit with a drink watching the sun go down. I don't have the talent to describe what I see, so will just leave you with this; the view looks unearthly, a magical scene not of this world, the dusky pink sky reflecting on the clear blue water below. If you dive in, you might be immersed in water or sky. It's a moment to take a breath and be grateful for the life I have.

That's it from me – I'm off to put on some aftersun on my predictably burnt shoulders and chest from having the window open all day – it's a must on a road trip! If you don't burn one arm, how can you claim to be on a road trip? Also, I'm knackered from being up early and its 10.30pm now. But, if I don't get these adventures on paper, I will have no chance of remembering them later. Time to close on another day. I've also kept a paper diary in which I jot down notes when I don't have my laptop to hand. Lucky you.

Accommodation: Pukenui Lodge Motel
Nights: 2
Number: 8
Type: Studio
Facilities: Hob, sink, microwave. Shower looks weird; but is very good
Price: £125.39
Wi-fi: Free and fast
Check-In: Fast, friendly and smooth
Parking: Right outside the studio and free
Weather: Some rain showers and cloud. Hot – between 21–24 degrees.

Skin Colour: Slight hint of pink followed by sunburn on one side... the joys of chilling in the car
Bites: None

Total Spent: *$150.84/£78*

Pukenui

Day 8 | Monday 25th February

We have a restful night as we were both tired after the long drive, and to be honest, I think we still have residues of jetlag. It hasn't been bad really, but the long flights do catch up with you at odd times, especially if you talk to people back home and the time zones are weird.

The morning doesn't exactly start out that well as I cannot find my sunglasses anywhere. I look in every bag about four times, check with the site office, ask at the shop. Chris goes to look around the picnic bench where we enjoyed the glorious sunset the night before. I give up, annoyed with myself that I've lost them, especially as a few times before I'd left the UK I'd wondered if I should take some spare ones – as mine are prescription glasses I cannot really just buy new ones off the shelf.

We are just about to set off in the car as we have decided to visit Cape Reinga which is at the top of the North Island and the reason for coming this far North.

Before we set off, me a little bit grumpy if I'm honest, as not having sunglasses is annoying when it's so sunny, and my glasses case came from my favourite city in Spain, Seville. I bought this when I was on holiday with mum, so it has fond memories attached to it. It's also not like me to lose things. *(Well other than gloves. I simply cannot keep hold of a pair of gloves.)* One last check in the studio reveals them to be under the covers of the bed, which we had both already checked. No doubt I had slept with them all night! I was going to make a reference to the princess and the pea, but right at this moment I cannot remember the story; I'm pretty sure she didn't sleep well though, and I did – so probably a rubbish comparison. Never mind.

> **TOP TIP:** *Get to Cape Reinga early. Bus trips come from places like Auckland and due to the time to travel there, they arrive around lunchtime, so if you can get there earlier you will get a quieter time to experience the breath-taking views and enjoy the whole vibe of the place. There are toilets at the top just before you walk down to the lighthouse.*

Finally, we set off and the weather is gorgeous, 22 degrees with wispy clouds dotting the sky. It soon dispels our frantic morning. It's approximately 10am so still enough time to get to the top before the pesky tourists. We decide to get some fuel just in case. Very conveniently located to the side of the Pukenui Lodge Motel is a little 'gas' pump as you go towards the dock area.

> **TOP TIP:** *If you're using your credit card it will take a deposit of $150 off your card as a holding fee until the transaction has gone through. The next day the $150 hold was taken off, and the transaction fee applied. So, this worked really well. But we didn't know this at the time; so it added to the stressful morning.*
>
> **TOP TIP:** *Get an LYK card or something similar. I read some negative reviews about the LYK card, but so far it's worked on contactless, in the ATMs and the pending activity for a payment shows straight away. So, it's useful for keeping track of what you've spent on the app. (Obviously since I've written this Thomas Cook went bust!)*

The TOP TIPs are flowing in this chapter! Almost feels like a proper travel journal.

Just before we finally leave… we fill up 27 litres in at $2.09, which cost $57.71. I've added the fuel details at the end in the aptly named 'fuel costs' for those petrol heads out there.

Finally, ready, we head to Cape Reinga. Once again on the drive we enjoy absolutely amazing views. This is why we came to New Zealand. Our perfect holidays are cruising in a car or on a motorbike, taking in the scenery. I don't care if I don't do any of the typical tourist events, this will do me right here. The light dances across the hillside and the sheer size of the landscape really is breath-taking – I think these are words I will use a lot about this wonderful island. Stop at every place you can to take pictures or drink in the views. This is an island to be enjoyed. Print those memories on your retina ready for a glum rainy day at home.

We drive North on the SH1 through Ngataki, Te Kao, stopping to take pictures when we can. In all of these areas where we have spent a mere one day exploring, you could stay a month and not see everything, so you really need to pick carefully the experiences you want to have in the time you have.

Cape Reinga is really worth a visit, it's at the very top of the island where the two seas meet; the South Pacific Ocean and the Tasman sea causing large waves. It's stunning, I will have to look up some more words to describe the scenery so you don't get bored. The sea is bluer than blue can be, the white crests crashing violently into the other body of water. They seem to be in a constant battle over their borders, a bit like humans.

Due to its location it's windy and feels cold at the top, but making our way down we enjoy the views and stop to read the information boards. We arrived at about 11ish, so there were maybe twenty people milling about. As I've said we were told it can get very crowded. We wondered if we needed coats, but you certainly don't need them when you walk back up.

There are many walks you can enjoy around this area like the Te Paki Coastal Track. You can see why they believe this is a spiritual place. It's easy to believe you're at the end of the earth, and all things in life are possible.

Feeling happy that we've made an effort to stray this far North, it is worth the drive. We return to our accommodation to make butties before heading out to a beach sign we had seen for Henderson Bay – wow wow wow wow, flipping heck: it's like being in Barbados, tropical beach, white sands, white waves breaking over a deep green sea – just wow. This is not to be missed. We loiter around for a while and wander the beach, enjoying the feel of the sand. It is tricky to climb back up to the top where we've parked the car, at one point I imagined us plunging to our deaths – possibly a little dramatic, but it is a bit hairy! I'm sure there must be a better way to get up and down. The road to this idyllic beach is strange, you go from tarmac, to gravel track and back again all the way, so be careful in a car.

After this, it is back to the studio for a shower. *(Reading that again it sounds like I'm a tv presenter!)* We get rid of the sand in our toes and freshen up. Then we make our way to the Ninety-mile beach, which is in about every guidebook as a must visit. I would say, yes, it is stunning, and in some areas of the beach you can do various water sports. I would choose Henderson's beach hands down. It depends what you're looking for. End of the day, it is each to their own. We prefer to be away from the crowds and do our own thing.

During this busy but fabulous day, we go to the shops and supermarkets which we do about three times a day, just because we like eating and keep forgetting stuff! This is precisely what we do at home, so this really is a home from home for us.

If I can share photos, I hope to show the sunset as I'm writing up this journal. I'm going to use wow again, I cannot help it! I think I will have to take a second mortgage to pay for all the photos we've taken so far. It will take a year to get them in order.

Right that's the day over with, and my journal is done. The sun has nearly set, and I'm looking forward to chilling and reading my book before bedtime. Tomorrow we move on from Pukenui to Whangarei for two nights – where we make a bit of a mistake with the accommodation…

Plans for the next few days include a boat trip at the Bay of Islands and visiting the Whangarei Falls, all being well.

Thoughts on Pukenui Lodge Motel – basic, but clean. There was a slightly musty smell coming from the cupboards in the kitchen area, but that didn't make the room smell. We took out the plates and bowls and washed them as the smell clung to them. Don't let this put you off though. The woman is friendly, and our room was cleaned while we were out. The location is better than we expected. Grab yourself a drink and sit on the benches overlooking the inlet and watch the sun go down – pure heaven. There is a well stocked 4 Square supermarket across the road, and a bar which does a good cappuccino for $4.50. You get a free parking spot next to the studio. The motel is extremely quiet at night, and they do have a sign up about noise, and it works as we didn't hear a peep. The studio is close to the road, but we couldn't hear a thing – although it's not as if there is much traffic about. It is New Zealand after all.

Total Spent: *$103.62/£54*

Pukenui to Whangarei
Day 9 | Tuesday 26th February

I wake up after, quite frankly, a shit night's sleep. My sunburn has a lot to do with it, despite the sun factor fifty I'd lathered on. I start the day feeling knackered and have a headache. But it's holiday time, so I have to get on with it. I feel a bit out of sorts all day until I relent and have an Ibuprofen when we arrive at the hotel. After about half an hour I feel better, which goes to prove the power of drugs is needed sometimes. Which reminds me… in Singapore Airport we got a piece of paper when we went through security which said, 'WARNING: DEATH FOR DRUG TRAFFICKERS UNDER SINGAPORE LAW'. I'm glad they don't class Ibuprofen as hard drugs. I wonder how they kill them? My overactive imagination has managed to think of many ways.

(I looked this up later and between 1994 -1998, Singapore had the second highest per capita execution rate estimated to be 13.83 people annually to each million.)

As I said yesterday, we made the mistake of booking a studio in Whangarei thinking it had cooking facilities, and it doesn't. It just adds that little extra cost as we have to eat out and it can be challenging to eat quite as healthy. We've avoided eating out so far though, so I suppose it will be nice to have a bit of a treat, as long as we keep an eye on the budget.

> **TOP TIP:** *Make sure you check your accommodation has cooking facilities. In the UK, I would say most accommodation classed as a studio would have some kind of cooking facility.*

After making butties, packing up and checking out, we make our way from Pukenui to Whangarei.

The blue skies are with us again as we travel through the Raetea and Maungataniwha Forests. Although the roads are not for the faint-hearted but they're simply stunning. The trees and foliage are sub-tropical, and you know you are in a different part of the world. The bends are sharp and steep, and Chris loves it. I'm sure he's pretending to be a rally driver. Drivers on the NZ roads are courteous, and even lorries move over where possible to let you pass. This behaviour is sadly very rare in the UK, where they are more likely to pull over into the next lane whilst going uphill to block your car. I'm sure they play games to try and annoy other drivers. In New Zealand, if you're in a slower vehicle, it's expected that you pull over when safe, and let faster road users go past.

We find a lovely waterfall on the Waitangi River, and stop to enjoy our packed lunch. It's well worth a stop. People are milling about and kayaking on the river; lots of cockerels are hanging about and making their presence known. There are plenty of tracks you can walk along to enjoy the woods and follow the river. Sadly, it's only a lunch break for us. The cool bags work a treat and I'm glad we decided to buy them when we arrived. Providing you have a fridge/freezer in your accommodation, even after a day in the car, Chris's beers are still cold, so he's happy.

(The cool bag made it back to the UK. Chris takes his packed lunch to work in it and we take it on any day trips. It's filled with butties and memories of New Zealand.)

Arriving in Paihia is magical, the bright green/blue waters with the islands dotted about are a sight to behold. I think Mother Nature really did surpass herself when she made

New Zealand. We stop here and park next to the sea. So far, parking seems to be free in NZ – which is something the UK should take note of – we charge for everything and it's far too expensive. It's certainly not the way to encourage tourism.

Back to basking in the views. We find the visitor's centre where I have a chat with a very helpful bloke who does us a good deal for tomorrows boat trip. We are going to visit Russell Island, and will then cruise around the bays to find the dolphins. So exciting.

Excursions booked, Chris has a dip in the sea while I read my book, although it's hard to concentrate with the views daring you to look again. Just one more glimpse. I manage a few pages before giving up and succumbing to the vista. After all, that is what a holiday is all about.

Reluctantly moving on from this idyllic place, we stop off en route to look at the Whangarei Falls, which is only a 1km detour from our hotel. You can park for free. The falls are easy to get to, as you simply walk down some steps from the car park and there they are, simply stunning. You can do a 30-minute quick walk to see them from a distance, or a 2.5-hour walk. I wish we had time to do the walks but I'm glad we decided to take a quick glimpse.

We arrive at our hotel for the next few nights. Discovery Settlers Hotel is how I imagine motels in America. The ones you see in the movies where the cars park outside, a large balcony wrapped all around the outside with white shutters to finish off the look. Check-in is the fastest yet. Hello, very friendly, key, wi-fi password and off we go. The room is clean and tidy as well as big and airy with a large bed. The TV is huge, not that we really watch it. But, as I've said, no cooking facilities.

After unpacking, which consists of putting our food in the freezer as it does have a mini fridge/freezer and opening the cases. We take the 10–15 minute walk into the town basin. What a lovely place and well worth the trail along the river. Cormorants are constantly diving in the river for dinner. Hungry ourselves we head to a place called The Dune, which is on the riverside and I recommend eating here.

It has stunning views of the boats on the river. Idyllic. I could sit here all day and watch the world go by. The pizza is particularly tasty with large chunky tomatoes and pesto. Delish. Overall with drinks and fries, it costs $46.50 about £25.

Whilst enjoying lunch, we comment that if the weather was this nice in the UK this place would be busier than a book signing for GRRM. Only 10–15 people are eating or passing the time with a drink. The waiters are very chatty and friendly, and we spend a few minutes talking with one who has visited London. I love the random little chats with people throughout life, being naturally very nosey I love hearing people's stories. Where they have come from? Where they are going? Why did they end up where they are? Life is fascinating. We leave feeling full and relaxed.

Deciding that we are ready to chill, we find the nearest supermarket for supplies. One thing we have observed, is how many people walk around barefoot over here whilst shopping. If we did that in the UK the security guards would probably be chucking us out. It seems acceptable and normal here. After a glance at one woman's feet, I suspect she would have to stand in bleach for two weeks to get them clean. Doesn't bother me, just an observation, not as if we eat food off the floor, but I don't think I will observe the five second rule if I drop food in here.

Today my thoughts have naturally turned to my dad. He died 18 years ago today. I still cannot believe it's been so long. He was my best friend as well as my dad. He was always one for adventure and trying new things, and I think he would be proud of what I'm doing now. When I got the call to say he'd had a heart attack, I lived 3.5 hours away by car, and I was told not to rush. It was a Monday evening and I'd had a shitty day at work.

That kind of phone call soon puts life into perspective. Anyway, I don't want to bring the mood down, this is more about saying that I'm doing what he would want me to do, and that's enjoying life. Also, life experiences naturally make you reminisce about times gone by.

Me signing off day nine in New Zealand. So far, it's not disappointing – not that I really thought it would be. If you love epic landscapes and views that change at every turn, then this is the place for you. Everyone has been very friendly – a bit like Ireland; last time we were in a supermarket there, a woman actually opened another checkout to serve us because we were waiting. Customer Service barring the odd person has disappeared in the UK. We have lots of policies about it, but the smile promised on paper doesn't often make it to the staff serving you.

We've realised that we've packed the tin opener from the last place we stayed… oops. We are now fugitives on the run… you may never hear from us again, or maybe we will be on the news? If this is my final statement, then New Zealand, it's been emotional.

Accommodation: Discovery Settlers Hotel – Whangarei
Nights: 2
Number: 46
Type: Standard Studio
Facilities: No cooking facilities. Outdoor swimming pool: Looks a bit murky, but won't have time to use it.
Price: £133.06
Wi-fi: Free and very fast
Check-In: Fast, no problems
Parking: Right outside the studio and free
Weather: Hot 21–24, welcome cloud in the afternoon.
Skin Colour: Deep lobster pink (I'm very thankful for the aftersun!)
Bites: None

Total Spent: *$71.50/£37*

P.S. So I'm not leaving this on a cliffhanger as I do in my novels… I've messaged the previous accommodation, and they said, 'Don't worry about the tin opener.' So, sadly we're not on the run, or going to be on TV. It would have made for a great story and probably sold more books – but never mind.

Day trip to Paihia
Day 10 | Wednesday 27th February

Today starts with a bit of stress again: not all dream holidays are a dream the whole time. Without giving too much away and risking you closing the book, I know I have an infection and need to see a doctor – cue… damn it, we're on holiday, what the hell do we do? After getting our stuff together as we've booked the boat trip at the Bay of Islands today, we find a pharmacy en route, and I speak to a lovely assistant who puts me at ease. She talks to the pharmacist, and they suggest I visit the Whitecross Centre. This is an emergency care centre, and they see foreign visitors. Basically, you pay approximately $115, and they give you the forms to claim back on your insurance. It could be an hour's wait, and we have to be at the Bay of Islands for our boat trip and also need to fill up on fuel, so we have to leave it for now. I feel better knowing there is access to a doctor if I need it. We get on the road and decide to worry about this later. There is no way I'm going to miss the boat trip so we just have to crack on.

Enjoying the stunning views en route, we arrive at the Bay of Islands which has plenty of toilets. *(Maybe I should have added a toilet to the front cover? But these amenities are important and hardly feature in any guide books. Bit like works of fiction where the characters never use the bathroom.)* There is an ATM across the road from the quayside to get some cash if you need it. There are quite a few gift shops as well if you have time to meander around.

As we come into Paihia we are stopped by the police and a road awareness group giving out leaflets about road safety and speed. I will say I haven't seen a speed camera yet; only one traffic speed van.

> **TOP TIP:** *Jumping on the fast ferry to Russell Island means you beat the crowds on the main ferry. You don't miss out on any views or the trip; it just means you arrive onto Russell Island quicker and have more time before you catch the main boat for your trip. More about this later.*

After catching the fast ferry we arrive onto Russell Island and settle down to enjoy our cappuccino on the stunning waterfront. This island is well worth a visit, we feel so chilled out, especially after the stressful morning. After our caffeine levels are topped up, we meander in no particular direction down Church Street, York Street and Wellington Street taking in the sights of this lovely place. They have some quaint gift shops and plenty of places to eat. I of course, a book lover, writer and ex-Library Assistant, find the island's library.

It's not a huge place but I could quite easily come here with a book and entertain myself with walks around the island, followed by a lazy read in the sunshine, listening to the waves quietly caressing the pebbles on the beach. Bliss.

Too quickly it's time to board the main boat; now if you want to get a prime seat up top or at the front, I suggest you board at the main port in Paihia and secure your seat, as there aren't many suitable spaces left for the people getting on at Russell Island. Since we've had a few long drives, we are happy to stand at the back of the boat for the duration, and we have a cunning plan…

The boat is on the verge of setting sail for home when we are eventually treated to a stunning display by the dolphins.

Lucky for us this won't be the first time we see them during our time in New Zealand. And thanks to our cunning plan, we are in the right place to have the best view of the dolphins – absolutely outstanding. New Zealand just keeps giving. How much more can there be?

The dolphins are spectacular. We stand. In awe, mouths open, watching their acrobatics. I think they might be showing off and rightly so. Seeing animals in the wild is undoubtedly the greatest pleasure in life.

I can highly recommend the boat trip. Again, I feel lost for the right words to describe the beauty of these islands, and we've seen only a fraction of them. The Bay of Islands is where a Maori voyager set foot, followed by Captain Cook, and the treaty of Waitangi was signed here. (*You can read about more detailed information on this if you visit the museum in Wellington.*)

Another stunning day and a pleasant drive back to Whangarei, we forage (*Go to the supermarket.*) and discover the fantastic salad counter which we will use quite a lot over this trip. They have some delicious concoctions of potato salads, quiche and lots of other pots of loveliness, add it to a salad bag and you have a healthy tea when you have no cooking facilities. They also do the best blueberry muffins – so light and tasty. They have plastic cutlery on the counter to buy at the salad bar; a bargain and useful when self-catering. Now, I know plastic is the 'big' talk of the town at the moment and so it should be. But rest assured we do recycle!

So far, every person we've come across has been friendly and polite, but I've listened in to a few conversations between locals, and they go something like this… (*Could I suggest you skim to the next page if you don't like swearing.*)

'Fucking, fuck, you had a good day?'
'Yeah, fuckin brilliant day, thanks mate.'
'Ah, brilliant mate.'
'See ya. Have a great fuckin' evening.'

I won't add the rest as you get the picture. This is all said in the friendliest manner possible.

Anyway, that's it. My sunburnt chest is hotter than the fires of Mordor. Going to spray myself and try to get some sleep ready for the long drive to Rotorua tomorrow and the inevitable trip to the doctors.

We will be visiting Hobbiton on Friday. Oh my God, I'm so excited.

Total Spent: $321.21/£167

The accountants and fellow Yorkshire folk will have seen the daily total, and an intake of breath would have followed. This is mainly due to the boat trip cost, which was worth every single penny. We've spent very little the few days prior to this to compensate for the touristy stuff. So, rest easy and put your calculator away as we are still not over budget.

Whangarei to Rotorua
Day 11 | Thursday 28th February

After not a bad night's kip, considering the sunburn and the ongoing medical problem, we get ready in record time, having now mastered the art of living out of suitcases.

It's a long drive today to Rotorua from our lovely stay in Whangarei, again another place we could spend longer; which is still the theme of the holiday in New Zealand. The drive today will be approximately five hours without stops. It will take us back past Auckland as we make our way to the 'stinky' place that is Rotorua – or so we've been warned.

As we drive through the beautiful tropical mountains, hugging the sides of the roads, we're joined by the constant noise of the cicadas *(Insects with wings.)*. During the summer they sing in chorus looking for a mate, and by the sound of the constant drone they are not having much luck in that department.

One thing that has surprised me is the number of cows in the North. *(I can tell you're regretting buying this now…)* after reading and watching various things about New Zealand, they all mention the sheep. Well, in the North it's the cow's domain. There are sheep, but we've not seen that many, but it could be that are living up in the hills. We pass a sign complaining about the number of cattle in the area, so maybe that explains a few things. There ends your information guide on the cattle in NZ, I wouldn't go looking for a 'Cattle Guide to New Zealand by C.L. Peache' anytime soon.

We have a few stops along the way; important if you need to use the restroom as much as I do.

When we arrived into the outskirts of Auckland earlier in the day, the bypass went on forever. It felt like it would never end and I would and at the age of 43, start wetting myself. Adding up the number of ailments we've had on this journey so far, it wouldn't have surprised me to be quite honest.

Anyway, you will be pleased to hear that I didn't wet myself and we managed to find a supermarket and grab some food for our lunch. The deli counter at the Countdown Supermarket is our staple diet, they are so good.

(Whenever we say Countdown, we have to do the theme tune to the TV programme. We cannot help it; believe me, we have tried.)

We pull off the main road called Araimus Road and find an idyllic place to sit and enjoy our salads. It's a lovely shaded layby with a chilled horse watching us munch our lunch, as he chews his. We turn to see a lady approaching the car. We smile, hoping we aren't going to get in trouble. There is a sign for grapes for sale in the layby, and she is coming from the house that sells them.

She says, "Just checking you're alright, the cars sometimes miss the ditch in the layby."

How lovely of her to check we're okay. We assure her we are fine and that we've stopped to enjoy the view and have lunch, and we all go about our day. The horse glances up once to watch the exchange, maybe wondering if it is going to get a treat.

The area from Auckland to Rotorua outside Waharoa is more sun-scorched than anywhere we've seen so far. We're surrounded by imposing mountains and the landscape looks like you're driving through a crater. On the subject of roads: they have been much better than we were led to believe, although there is a heck of a lot of roadworks going on.

It looks like they are investing heavily in roads and infrastructure for trains, although we have only seen one freight train full of logs so far. For some reason we thought we would see more.

I will mention the places we drove through courtesy of the iPhone locations, as I love to see places I've visited and when you're on the road you cannot take note of everywhere you pass as you're busy looking at the scenery, or ideally the road if you're the driver. Here goes; Ruakaka, Waipu, Topuni, Wellsford, Sheep world, Northcote, Westhaven (this is driving through Auckland), Drury – where we have an encounter with a friendly lady, Bombay (not a detour), Ngarua, Matamata, Waharoa – home to Griddle Earth Café *(lol)*, Tapapa, Hamurana, before finally arriving into a not as smelly as we were led to believe; Rotorua. Pronounced Rota-roo-a.

Arriving into the outskirts of Rotorua I start sniffing and sniffing, expecting the over-powering eggy smell. Fifteen minutes later and light-headed from sniffing, it still hasn't hit me. I'm generally sensitive to smells, not like Chris who barely has a sense of smell at all and probably is the kind of person this place should be encouraging to live here. We arrive at our motel for the night, and it's only then I detect a faint hint of something in the air.

After checking in, we gratefully get out of the sun and into the apartment. Coming from zero degrees in the UK to this weather has been a shock to my poor pale body, especially as I didn't read the label on the suncream, which said to rub it in. I bought spray to save getting greasy hands. I've paid for my stupidly and not reading the label – I should know better at my age.

Chris has come down with a cold, so we've stocked up on Sudafed and Lemsips at the cost of £17; not in our budget, but I nearly had to spend $177 at the doctors the other day, and I won't begrudge him medicine.

I might need to pay for some skin grafts if I get any more burnt! Bloody sun.

Anyway, I've used the facilities at the motel – I know what you're thinking but this time it's the washing facilities. It's $8, which is about £4 for a wash and dry so not so bad. All easy to use and again feels like we live here because we're doing the mundane things of home. After the daily trip to the supermarket, we fill up the car with fuel ready for tomorrow – my Hobbiton visit – I'm so excited, and the weather looks perfect. As much as I moan about the heat and my sunburn, we've been lucky enough to have excellent weather for all our activities.

The day closes on another fantastic drive through New Zealand and despite Chris's cold, my sunburn and dodgy bits, *(Which will involve the trip to the docs I've tried to avoid.)* this trip is bloody amazing so far.

We're not the going 'out-out' kind on holidays. We tend to get up early, explore and take in the vibes, so now we find ourselves chilling in the room after a dip in the hot tub that comes with our apartment. Life is pretty darn good.

Accommodation: Geneva Motor Lodge – Rotorua
Nights: 2
Number: 3
Type: Studio with hot tub
Facilities: Microwave, fridge, general kitchen facilities. Hot Tub – which is amazing
Price: £157.97
Wi-fi: Free and very fast
Check-In: Fast, no problems 3% charge for using a credit card
Parking: Right outside the studio and free
Weather: Hot 21–25, welcome cloud in the morning
Skin Colour: Robin red breast, partly due to sun and party due to the red rash I've developed because I have an infection. Great. I will probably be quarantined if any officials catch up with me!
Bites: None

Total Spent: *$172.46/£90*

Hobbiton!

Day 12 | Friday 1st March

We get up early for our very exciting pre-booked visit to Hobbiton. So excited! It's approximately an hour's drive from Rotorua on some very scenic – of course it's scenic… it's New Zealand after all. My health problem isn't getting better, so the plan is to visit the doctors after Hobbiton. Nothing short of death will stop this visit today. Amazing how you can ignore these things when having fun.

I don't know how many times I've seen and read the *Lord of the Rings/Hobbit*, possibly pushing 50? Well, I've watched LOTR more than I've read it and read The Hobbit more than I've watched the films. I've also listened to the audiobooks – so you could say I'm a bit of a fan.

Hobbiton did not disappoint, in fact, it exceeded my expectations. The tour is just over 2 hours long and you get loads of time to take pictures and enjoy the world of the Hobbits. The tour guide is very knowledgeable and makes the tour very interesting, with lots of snippets of information about behind the scene shots and the way the world was created for film.

I could have quite easily hung around all day, just enjoying the feeling of the place, it is so chilled. Again, we are fortunate with the weather, it's cloudy and about 20 degrees, so perfect for wandering around and enjoying this idyllic slice of the world. I've ticked this off the bucket list but added a footnote to come back again. I heard one of the guides saying that they were looking for tour guides. Where is the application form? What a job!

If you're thinking of coming to New Zealand, then Hobbiton is an absolute must. Plenty of people were on the tour who were not LOTR fans – heathens – same as some people who haven't watched Walking Dead or Game of Thrones *(Roll of the eyes.)*.

I would suggest you book way in advance if you only have a small window of time to visit as we did; you don't want to be disappointed and miss out if they are fully booked.

The drink out of a stone flagon in the Green Dragon is a highlight. They have a roaring fire in the mega hearths – magical. I want to move in. We leave feeling very happy and keen to go back – always a good sign. It would make an excellent writing retreat and would certainly get the creative juices flowing.

After this fabulous visit, we make our way back to our accommodation in Rotorua for lunch. As I've said before, we are trying to spend as little as possible on shopping, so we have enough money for any events we want to do. But, more so, this trip is about getting out on the road and enjoying the country. Once we've had lunch, I succumb to the inevitable trip to the doctors to sort out my waterworks. I know by now that I need antibiotics, the rash on my face is a clear indication it isn't just going to go away – sigh.

I have to say the staff at the medical centre are great. Basically, I pay a flat fee of $177 to see the doctor. A girl who is training to be a medical practitioner sees me first, all part of learning the ropes. We have a lovely chat. I pee in a bowl, and she confirms I have an infection. I wait to see the doctor and get a prescription for my drugs – these cost $15, so all told about £100. It's worth it, as I'm not going to get better on my own. The whole service is excellent, and I feel fortunate to be able to communicate easily; it's obviously not so easy in some countries. I would say all in all it took about an hour. Anyway, we will have to take the hit for this as my insurance excess is £175.

I have to take 4 tablets a day for 5 days and no drinking alcohol – it's Friday night! Gutted. Chris says, 'Why don't you just take them all?' *(Insert eye roll)*. Because, my darling, that is called an overdose! Maybe he's had enough of me and my medical problems. Even with all these little events, we still haven't argued, so that's got to be good.

> **TOP TIP:** *Make sure you check the medical excess on your policy before you buy.*

After all this messing about we go on a drive and stop around Lake Rotorua, some stunning locations to pull over and enjoy the mountains and views across Tahuna-a-Pukeko – Hamurana Lakefront Reserve and Puhirua Bay. Lots of wildlife hanging about; including black swans. Having to visit the doctors in another country is a bit stressful so it's nice to take a moment out of the day to re-relax.

After the drive we chill in the room since we are both a little delicate health wise. Although to be fair, we are not night people on holidays, as I've said before. This is about the long game. It's the first of March today, and the tour guide at Hobbiton told us that today is their first day of Autumn, which seems weird since in the UK we are waiting for Spring to arrive. The UK saw some record-breaking good weather earlier in the week, although they have now gone back to usual temperatures of 7–9 degrees in the day and 3 at night, which feels sub-zero when at home.

We try to top-up my Lyk card with more NZ money, which proves a bit of a faff as my bank send authorisation codes to my old sim number. So, Chris has to put my sim card in his phone and then it still doesn't work. *(We leave it until the next day and do exactly the same thing and it works fine, so maybe it was just the wi-fi.)*

I still have to put my UK Sim into the phone for transfer from the bank to work, so worth bearing in mind that you need to authenticate transfers.

Time to sign off now after a day I will never forget. Tomorrow we have a few breaks planned on the way to Napier, where we will stay one night before moving onto Wellington and then crossing to the South. I cannot believe we are nearly two weeks into our trip. Fingers crossed the time left will be illness-free.

If I ever come back to NZ again, and I've won the lottery, I would do a week in all the places and probably still not see everything, although you could say this about areas in the UK. There are so many beautiful locations to visit in the UK, but somehow it makes you feel like more of an explorer when you take a flight to far off lands.

I've checked my Hobbiton photos, and I've taken over one hundred and fifty, and that's just with my phone, not including the ones on the camera. I will upload my photos onto my website and I will try and be selective or else you might want to book the day off work to go through them.

Total Spent: *$400.47/£208*

Sorry, I know certain fellow Yorkshire folk are sucking in air again. Today's high cost is due to the Hobbiton Trip, which we booked in advance from the UK and my medical expenses. It's worth keeping a contingency fund for unexpected payments.

Rotorua to Napier
Day 13 | Saturday 2nd March

Early to bed, early to rise. We're all packed up and ready to leave before 9am. We've enjoyed our stay in Rotorua, and luckily for us, it hasn't been that smelly.

We decide to try out the Go Pro in the car and film the journey from Rotorua to Napier. Chris tells me to keep quiet as he's recording and immediately I want to start talking, I cannot help myself. The footage comes out really well, so that's our Friday nights sorted when back at home. We will kick back with a drink and watch our road trip videos and look at thousands of pictures.

The journey is another epic one – I don't think New Zealand can manage anything less. The dense forests permeate the route from Taupo to Napier, the ground changing from the sandy dunes to hard rocks. Some of the scenery is similar to the Swiss Alps. They look like managed forests, and remote random houses sit in the wilderness, and you cannot help but wonder who lives there. Obviously, my mind makes up something suitably scary; imagining serial killers waiting to prey on broken down drivers…

It's worth stopping off at a place called Tahorakuri Forest, even if it's just to snap a picture. Beautiful turquoise coloured waterfalls and lakes are surrounded by trees; heartbreakingly beautiful. Waipunga also has a stunning waterfall. I guess these will all depend on rainfall/time of year though. I can see why so many films are made in New Zealand. It must be a dream to shoot films on this island, the epic landscape doing all the work for you.

There are plenty of brown tourist signs on the road to Napier, but due to time, we cannot stop at all of them.

We plan to stop and look around Taupo after a friend recommended it, but a cycling event has shut off a lot of the roads, so we enjoy the view from afar and carry on our journey to Napier after a frustrating weave through many closed off roads. What would a road trip be without a diversion?

Once we've checked into BK Fountain Court and emptied our bags, we wander into Napier, and are treated to perfect weather. I slip on my leggings, light top and cardigan. We feel like we've arrived on a Bank Holiday. It's 4pm on a Saturday and there is hardly anyone about, which is true of much of New Zealand though, other than the big places like Auckland. It feels like the whole infrastructure has been put in place and it's just patiently waiting for the people to arrive. Maybe it's the time of year? Perhaps in the height of summer the place is buzzing – but it doesn't feel like it will be that way. To us, it's perfection, but you wonder how the shops make their money.

Napier is very pleasant and very clean. They had a devastating earthquake in 1937 and it's been rebuilt in the Art Deco style – it suits it. Even though we have never been to America, so much of New Zealand reminds us of places we see on tv, and how you imagine it to be. Some of the buildings are stunning. I'm not a massive fan of Art Deco, but even if it's not your thing, I'm sure you'll be impressed by what they've achieved here. The Daily Telegraph building is particularly stunning, as is the Masonic Lodge.

We stop off at a pub which is a mixture of a Wetherspoons and an Irish bar back home. Funny how you gravitate towards things you recognise. Normally, we wouldn't bother but it seems to be one of the only lively places, which we discover is full of interesting characters, very much like some of the pubs back home.

Drink hastily consumed as we avoid a conversation with a chap who is obviously an 'interesting local character' we move on and find a lovely bar down the side of an alley and sit outside to enjoy the sunshine that is peeking over the buildings.

After our drinks and another little wander around, we find a fab chip shop 2 minutes from our accommodation. Very tasty, and it only cost, £3.50 for fish and chips. The fish is comparable to a small fish at home. Even though it's not Fish Friday we simply cannot pass up this opportunity and the BK Fountain Lodge Motel room isn't set up that well for cooking. After our tea, we find the beach to walk off the meal. Chris tries to get a beer from a corner shop but they don't sell it – one disappointed Other Half.

The beach in Napier is pebbly, the crashing green and white waves sound majestic against the backdrop of the cliffs in the distance, it really is a delight to walk along the seafront. As we meander, I think about all the places we've stayed so far.

All the accommodation has been different. Even though this studio is tired around the edges, everything is chipped and worn, but it's big enough and – bonus – it has four pillows. So many rooms seem to only have 3 pillows. I don't get it. One each and we share one? What's the deal with that? We haven't paid a fortune for our accommodation overall per night; there are only a couple that are near the £100 per night. Obviously, this is all down to personal budget. I would say most of ours are middle ground. If they lack something in the décor, it's made up for in location or views.

> **TOP TIP:** *Just double check with the accommodation to make sure it has what you need with regards to cooking facilities. Many seem to only have a microwave, kettle and toaster and no hob. Also, a lot say no to cooking strong smelling food in them, e.g. curries, fish etc. It limits what you can cook if you only have a microwave and cannot cook smelly food!*

So, far we have managed okay, and planned our dinners accordingly. We knew this Motel only had basic cooking facilities, so we had to have the take-away fish and chips. Had to! Which we enjoyed sitting on our rustic or rusty garden table and chairs overlooking the car park, with the sunshine that always seems to make an appearance at the end of the day.

After our beach walk and maybe two chips burned off in terms of calories, Chris plugs his tablet into the tv so we can watch a film on Netflix. It gives us something to do to while away the evening hours after a long day's driving. Generally, the TV channels are pretty basic here. End of the day, we're not here to watch TV, but a well-placed film at night while you're chilling out does no harm.

Tomorrow we head to Wellington and our last two nights in the North. The North has delivered the goods in terms of epic landscapes, friendly people and interesting places. It's day 13/14 on the road depending on the flights. I'm still unable to get my head around the times... our first fortnight done. I wasn't sure how I would take to being on the road for a long time. We've been lucky enough to have lots of holidays, and during our motorbike trip to Amsterdam we'd arrive, unpack, enjoy the holiday, pack and go home. This has been our first experience of living out of cases – if you're organised it's easy. We bought a bike lock which we fit around all our luggage when it's in the car. It just adds that bit of security to deter any thieves; everywhere has them, but NZ feels like a very safe place.

Accommodation: BK Fountain Court – Napier
Nights: 1
Number: 4
Type: Executive Studio
Facilities: Kitchenette, microwave. Spa bath: underwhelming
Price: £70.16
Wi-fi: Free and very fast
Check-In: Fast, no problems
Parking: Outside and free

Weather: About 14–16 and cloudy until we hit Napier, then rose to 19 degrees and mostly cloudy which is welcome relief to my skin.

Skin Colour: Robin red breast

Bites: None

Alcohol: NONE allowed due to drugs

Nail Varnish Remover: My search started a few days ago, and it is proving tricky to find some.

Total Spent: *$77.59/£40*

Napier to Wellington
Day 14 | Sunday 3rd March

Today we pack up and leave our very basic and tired apartment, although I will say the bed was very comfy and the neighbours were quiet, so this all resulted in a good kip. There are always positives if you want to find them.

It's a different kind of landscape on this trip, other than the surrounding mountains, we often feel like we are driving through Lincolnshire. In Pakipaki it's all flat grassland with cattle grazing, until we hit the mountain passes of Poukawa and Dannevirke, and we're back to the Derbyshire Dales with the odd palm tree chucked into the landscape. Some beautiful gravelly rivers pop up in between the trees through a place called Woodville, the water looking very inviting. We find a random white horse in a field that looks like Shadowfax. All the rivers we've seen seem very low, so I don't think the promised white-water rafting will go on in these places.

Cruising through one of the towns we stop to have a break and they have a lovely car boot and craft market at the side of the road. So many interesting bits and bobs it feels more like being at home. We purchase a couple of items from a stall and really like the look of a hessian sack which has held coffee at some point in its life and has writing all over it. As we chat about a potential problem with customs, or, more to the point, fitting it in our case, the owner starts chatting to us. We say why we were hesitating, and he says, 'Tell you what – have it for free and then if it gets taken off you it's no worries.' How amazing is that? The NZ folk really are nice people. So, we buy a couple of small items from him and leave feeling the love of New Zealand folk.

(The hessian sack made it home and currently has pride of place on the kitchen wall.)

One area we travel though has lots of white butterflies covering the bushes by the side of the road. There must be hundreds, if not thousands of them. I don't know if it's their day to breed or if they are just enjoying the sunshine but I'm sure that Chris's friend from McDonalds would know, and maybe he would oblige with the coffee grounds.

A good while out of Wellington the traffic is on stand still on the opposite side of the road. When we check later, we find it's due to an Eminem concert that took place last night. I hope they all had aircon in their cars due to the roasting conditions today. We realise why the North was so empty of people! They were all in Wellington, for one of the biggest names they've ever had.

Once we've checked into Marksman Motor Inn in Wellington, our home for the next two nights, we go for a wander into Wellington. Our Motel is in a great location, and is only a 10-minute walk to the Harbourside. This weekend seems to have been the busiest ever for Wellington with the Eminem concert. There are pop up art venues – quite frankly most of them are a bit weird for my taste: one woman sitting in something that looks like a swan and people are rubbing her with stuff; each to your own. I obviously don't have the creativity to understand that one! It's a really nice vibe though, lots of people chilling out and enjoying the nice weather. Hardly any wind in windy Wellington – I cannot believe it. I've packed on at least 7lb so far on the trip – purely so I didn't get blown away in Windy Welly... all the best laid plans.

We find a nice bar and head in for some food, this is our first proper sit-down meal in a pub, and we are not disappointed.

I go for a burger with all the trimmings, gherkins, tomato, bacon, loads of cheese, and Chris goes for a veggie burger. Since Chris is a Veggie, I don't tend to have very much meat, but every so often I love a good burger and this one is amazing. I keep struggling with the price conversion when paying for things though. It costs us $54 for two burgers, and Chris has a beer – I keep thinking, bloody hell £54 until I realise it's NZD and that equates to approximately £28, in a nice Quay/Harbour side location in a main city, you would be looking at double that in the UK.

Again, I cannot help but make comparisons to the UK; I think we basically rip off everyone… for everything. I feel very sorry for tourists visiting the UK. I bet they cannot believe that they get charged for everything. Whereas over here you feel they only charge you if they have to, if they can offer it for free then they do. Obviously not food and drink that would be business suicide, but parking might be a start. I suppose most of the main museums in the UK are generally free to enter – there, I said one good thing about the UK. They will be employing me on the tourist board before you know it!

It's a lovely start to our stay in Wellington. It's got a nice atmosphere, although it's certainly strange arriving in a place that's so busy. We are not used to seeing so many humans in one place.

Again, with the accommodation, make sure you check that they have what you need. This one hasn't even got a sink in the kitchen area. Basically, it should be called a double room with a toaster and microwave, I'm not sure a studio reflects the facilities. If it says kitchenette it should have the basics. It meant an interesting experience of washing and drying up in the bathroom – it even got Chris washing up – might get rid of the sink in the kitchen at home if it has this effect.

Time to get some sleep after a long but very enjoyable day.

Accommodation: Marksman Motor Inn – Wellington

Nights: 2

Number: 17

Type: Standard Studio

Facilities: Microwave, toaster. Strangely no separate sink – needed to use the one in the bathroom. Overall very clean and tidy. Extra touches like a bottle of milk, and toothbrushes. Nice large apartment.

Price: £163.01

Wi-fi: Free and fast

Check-In: Fast, no problems

Parking: Outside and free, but be careful with parking on this one, as they say on the website that they have parking, but it only has 14 spaces and more apartments than spaces, so first come first served.

Weather: About 16 degrees and not much cloud the whole day, started to rise to about 21/22 as the day went on.

Skin colour: Much better, more of a tan than a face full of rash and sunburn – result.

Bites: None

Alcohol: NONE (Sad face again.)

Nail Varnish Remover: Nope, nothing, nada

Total Spent: *$146.79/£76*

A day in Wellington
Day 15 | Monday 4th March

Thank God for being twelve hours ahead of the UK. I was going to message my nephew who turned 13 on the 3rd March but it was too early over there and then we were out and about, and okay, I will admit, then I forgot! You busted me. Anyway because of the time difference I'm still in time – RESULT – thanks NZ.

Another deep and comfy sleep; the beds and pillows over here are generally a lot comfier than the ones at home. We've been lucky enough to stay in a lot of hotels around the UK and abroad and I honestly don't know how they get it so wrong. Although most hotels abroad seem to have long thin pillows made of some kind of concrete. I think they must have investments in the local physios after their guests wake up with lopsided necks. Even being close to the road, it was a quiet night. Although that could be because I went into a coma due to being tired, and the drugs doing their job.

We head out for the morning and find a nice little coffee shop. Our caffeine levels topped up, we make our way to the Museum of New Zealand; Te Papa Tonga.

The museum is free, and a must do on your list. The information on the Maori history is amazing. We have lunch here which is cheap and very tasty.

Luckily for us there is a special event on – The Terracotta Warrior Guardians of Immortality at a cost of $19.50. I put my foot down and say we ARE paying for admission. Chris concedes as the moths fly out of his wallet. I have to do this if I want my own way when it comes to paying for stuff. You would think Chris was from Yorkshire and not me! It's well worth a visit and I'm really glad we make the effort. In general, this is a fab museum, so much information, and light and airy; an absolute pleasure to walk around.

I love taking quiet moments in a museum where you look at a piece properly and realise the age and the life experiences that object has had. I like to imagine the person making it. What did they think? Who did they make it for? They wouldn't have ever imagined a tourist looking at it at the other side of the world, in another time so different to their own. It blows the mind.

After this, we have a mooch around Wellington, making time for another coffee stop. The woman in the Bagel Café is very friendly; she likes the lime colour of my Lyk card. Amazing what can start a conversation. We feed our addiction before moving on to the cable cars. These cost $9 for a return or you can get a single for $5 and walk back down through the Botanical Gardens. We get a return. If we'd had more time, we would have walked the roughly 40-minutes back down through the beautiful gardens. But today is a whistle stop tour of Wellington. In the gift shop I persuade Chris to let me buy a bracelet. At this point I've decided he's got serious sunstroke, as he doesn't seem to be putting up a fight at all today. Normally, I get talked out of these things. If he reads this, I will get into trouble for painting him as a tight, controlling Gallah! To be fair, I'm a woman and our spending habits sometimes have to be controlled! Sorry to all other woman out there whose blokes are reading this; but, come on, it is true. Okay, I don't like to generalise, so let's say some people.

The Botanical Gardens are beautiful, and the views are suitably breath-taking. Tourists position themselves to take the perfect selfie, smiling 'the holiday' smile. I'm having a good time – even if they are not once the camera is removed from their face. Family and friends will have to endure endless pictures I've been taking. *(150 something at Hobbiton don't forget!)*

It's so beautiful up here. We exchange a few minutes' conversation with a couple who have that strong Yorkshire accent; how mine used to be before I moved around and about the UK. We discuss the noise of the pesky cicadas; the sound is almost deafening up here, but they are hard to spot. I'm pointing my camera at one and she takes my place to get a picture. We exchange information about them, and decide the males are clearly having no luck attracting a female as they haven't shut up to mate! We all share a giggle and go on our way.

Again, a visit is a must and at hardly any cost. We slowly make our way to the other Wellington Museum and after about half an hour we declare we have museum legs – basically tired from stopping and starting. Our highly tuned sense of direction takes us to a pub on the Harbour side for some beer battered chips; I'm still trying to put on weight in case the wind picks up – it's a brilliant excuse! We pass a boat which is covered in graffiti of sea gulls which is very cool; just like this city. We chill watching the world go by, and a seagull that is very protective over what it's designated as its area in front of the bar. It chases others at a speed Jessica Innis-Hill would be envious of. We find it a highly entertaining way to pass the time.

Deciding we need a proper rest, we make our way back to the apartment, where I'm now sitting typing up the day's events. Thank God I decided to do this; absolutely no way would I remember so much detail when we get home.

My antibiotics seem to be doing the trick and my problems, as well as my face, seem to be on the mend. So, tomorrow I will be leaving the North in better health, lots of fond memories of an amazing place, with friendly people and a whole lot more to explore given another lifetime.

After a rest we go to the supermarket, on the new mission... Since we arrived in New Zealand, I've been trying to buy nail polish remover. So far, no luck! Another fruitless search in the Countdown Supermarket, our preferred place over here to shop. This results in me having to sing 'The Final Countdown' and Chris humming the TV Countdown music, dada, dada da da da dah, or something like that. I must admit to forgetting to look a couple of times for the remover when out and about, it's only when I glance at my peeling nails at the end of the day, I think… bugger. Anyway, the search continues.

Walking to the supermarket takes us past some of the suburbs of the city, very interesting to see how people live, and I can see why some people compare it to San Francisco –the hills are very steep, and it gets the old calf muscles burning.

It's time to go down South and an early start to get our ferry, so another quick and worthwhile mention about the parking for this accommodation. When I told the owner we were leaving early, they advised us to move the car as people often block others in. So, where it might seem there are lots of spaces – you might find yourself blocked in when you try to leave in the early hours. She was right, and it was a good job I spoke to her and we moved the car. Anyway, we both had the inevitable dreams about cars blocking us in. We are due to be up at 6am, so it's off to bed. It's been a long but very pleasant day.

The North – it's been emotional.

Total Spent: *$184.28/£96*

Part Three: The South

North to South
Day 16 | Tuesday 5th March

I'm currently surrounded by the thousand-mile stare, the look of people who have had to get up too early to catch the 8am ferry to Picton only to be faced with an hour's delay. An hour they clearly feel they could have put to better use in their beds. At least we are treated to a lovely sunrise to while away the time. I ring my mum for a little mother/daughter time.

To get your boarding pass for the boat go to the desk inside the building. You show them the booking details on my phone, and they give you three boarding cards which you hand over to the staff as you park and board. Finally boarded, the ship makes its way out of the harbour, a fairly smooth departure. The views of the Cook Strait are beautiful, with a distant mist rising off the mountains. I'm surrounded by the wonderful smell of breakfast. I succumb to eating my prepared lunch cob and turn it into a second breakfast – memories of Hobbiton still with me.

The majestic mountains reveal themselves as we move through the strait; we are surrounded, with no way out. Every turn of the boat reveals another epic set of forest clad mountains. The unpaved highway of the sea leads us out to the ocean and the crossing to the South- island, waiting to show us its delights, while we wait to see if it can compete with the North. (*It can.*)

The crossing is approximately three and half hours. So, I'm going to use the time wisely, after my journal entry I will be turning my attention to my Christmas novella. Time to see what the characters have been up to while I've been away. Now available on my website… shameless plug!

There are many houses to the right of the boat as we leave Wellington, with no homes I can see on the left, houses that must only be able to be reached by sea and seem so remote the people living there must really need to get away from life. Remoteness is something people here must enjoy or have to get used to very quickly. I must admit after coming from the quiet of some of the places, it was strange to come back into the hustle and bustle of a city and I craved the peace and quiet.

On the boat we are treated to a group of children singing a Haka on the top deck. It gives me goose bumps, and what a way to transition from the North to the South. After a stunning journey across the straits, we cruise into the lands of the South. Arriving into Picton is how I imagine travelling through the Norwegian fjords to be. Absolutely stunning.

We disembark without problems and start our journey from Picton to Murchison. So much of the time spent on the road is completely traffic free. It seems only right to give a slight wave or nod at any passing car. We quickly run out of water as we didn't stop at the four-square supermarket in Picton and its hot today.

> **TOP TIP:** *Stop and get some supplies when you get off the ferry. There are plenty of places, we just didn't think to stop at any!*

At one point I'm seriously considering what I will do if I get stuck out here and desperately try to remember what Ed Stafford or Ray Mears would do when they run out of water. I don't fancy drinking my own wee since the antibiotic made it look like it had turned fluorescent yellow – yes, I know too much information about wee again! But, this is a real guide.

I wonder how long the bags of crisps will last, and how many days you can live on half an onion, when we spot a sign which promises delicious ice-cream – beware – on the day we passed it was shut or maybe a mirage... We continue up the road, with our mouths getting ever dryer, but still gasping and wowing at the epicness of the South.

On the outskirts of Picton are hundreds, if not thousands of rows of vines. Vineyards cover the whole area. I'm not surprised as it's very flat and roasting hot – 29 degrees the car shows. I find myself mesmerised by the perfect gaps between the rows: it's like looking through a kaleidoscope of images, houses cut into sections, jigsaw pieces waiting to be put together. This could just be the dehydration, and I wonder at the time if I can cut up a vine and drink it.

Chris is fast asleep, (Not in the car – this is me writing later in the day!) so I'm making the most of the time to catch up with my journal. I've left my Christmas novella at a tense point after managing 2,500 words on the ferry. I want to get back to that but need to write this up. I'm sitting here on a veranda, with a beautiful breeze blowing which is raising goose bumps on my arms, listening to the trickle of water from the water feature next to our motel room. The forest mountains are the backdrop, with horses neighing and grazing in the fields. Idyllic is the word I will use to describe this view and my feelings.

Anyhow, back to us eyeing each other up for food and drink in the car and wondering if the beer we have in the back counts as water. We come to a small place called Saint Arnaud. Maybe we've left it too long and it's another mirage, but no, this is a real heavenly place and I raise a cappuccino in thanks after gulping down a load of water.

We sit in a shaded picnic area and enjoy a well needed refreshment stop.

We move on, both glad we didn't have to eat each other or drink our own fluids. We buy a couple of bottles of water to keep us going; learning from our earlier error. We drive on marvelling at the landscape and meandering rivers as we arrive at our stop for the night; Mataki Motel in Murchison.

I'm greeted by a lovely host and given some milk in a ceramic jug with cling film on top – how quaint.

The room is also quaint; again no cooker or sink in the kitchenette, but a microwave and fridge. Why would you have a sink when you can wash up in the shower?

As I said earlier, at this point I had to stop writing for a few moments to enjoy the vista: the trees in front of the room are creaking and the wind is rustling through the leaves and bees buzzing about trying to get some food for the hive. These are the moments that life is all about. Simple pleasures, memories and feelings that I will remember long after the holiday is finished.

Even though we are tired, we go for a little walk around the town – which oozes quaintness. In the local store, I'm amazed by the array of hunting magazines in the small shop. They have tempting reduced Christmas food in a basket. After buying supplies, we walk down a little road to the left of our hotel. It leads to Matakitaki River – wow, absolutely stunning backdrop. Huge boulders line the sides of the river, the calmness belies the strength of this river, heavy with rainfall. I can easily picture people white water rafting here. The mountains in the distance create the perfect picture postcard of New Zealand. What a pleasure to behold such beauty.

Right, bringing this day to a close, after an interrupted night: it would be the only night we had some slightly noisy neighbours; of course I would have slept through it but Chris thought I needed to be woken up to tell me they were noisy – his version is slightly different.

Tomorrow we drive on through what I suspect will be even more epic scenery. Even our pictures won't do the vistas justice.

Accommodation: Mataki Motel – Murchison
Nights: 1
Number: 10
Type: Standard Studio
Facilities: Fridge, microwave, toaster. Again, no separate sink –

needed to use the shower and washing up bowl as the sink in the bathroom is too small. Overall very clean and tidy. It has a small wardrobe doors which open into the bathroom. I'm disappointed as I wanted it to lead to Narnia.

Price: £64.36

Wi-fi: Free and fast

Check-In: Fast, no problems

Parking: Right outside, plenty of spaces

Weather: About 29 degrees at the highest, approx. 21 in Murchison with a breeze; lovely temp to walk around the town.

Skin colour: I definitely have a tan, with some flaking, but the most normal I've looked in two weeks. Good job I don't do selfies – the filter I would have to apply would be off the scale!

Bites: None

Alcohol: You guessed it, still not allowed

Nail Varnish Remover: The search continues in the South... What is it with the lack of remover – does no-one paint their nails in NZ?

Total Spent: *£90.53/£47*

Murchison to Karamea
Day 17 | Wednesday 6th March

We wake to mountains shrouded in mist, and after breakfast go for a little walk to the riverside again. Moorhens, sheep and various other creatures are hanging about enjoying their breakfast. I highly recommend a walk around Murchison; what an interesting place, it's like going back in time. Quaint is the best word to describe it, you get the feeling it's very traditional. Everyone seems to know each other, and kids call out to 'Mrs Peterson' driving past in the car while they run home bare foot with some takeaway food. We indulge in a fabulous cappuccino at the Rivers café in the morning before heading off. The pies and desserts look amazing. (Don't say I didn't warn your waistline!) They have a constant stream of people coming in for them. I'm not quite sure where all these people are coming from though.

> **TOP TIP:** *When you do your shopping make sure you buy a sharp knife; these are blunt for one of three reasons: 1) In case the guests have annoyed each other and if they haven't got any sharp weapons they are unlikely to kill each other. 2) Most motels don't want you cooking things with strong smells e.g. fish – so a blunt knife isn't going to be of much use preparing fish or meat. 3) They never check if they have gone blunt.*

After breakfast we pack up and set off to Karamea. There are a lot of road works going on at the moment. The road workers are very polite. We cross a bridge and they all smile and wave and say thanks for waiting. In the UK they would be more likely to make you wait longer whilst they had their fag break – okay I know another sweeping generalisation – sorry to the proper hard-working road folk of the UK, but generalisations do appear for a reason in some cases.

At home, you will find miles and miles of traffic cones doing nothing other than slowing down the traffic and annoying everyone with their stubborn reflective presence.

The forest road is stunningly beautiful, especially with the cloud cover. Misty mountains indeed. It really sets the atmosphere for the drive. As I've mentioned before, the truck drivers actually move over and let you pass. The first time one did it we thought they were having a joke, but no, they actually do move over. It seems a couple of blasts of the horn as you pass is the way to say thanks.

Arriving into Karamea, the low cloud has created some fine rain and mist in the air. After checking in and we find yet another kitchen with only a microwave – but this one has a full-size sink. Hurrah! We drive to the beach, which is stunning and we only need share it with the seagulls.

The weather is against us today, but luckily, we don't mind. We didn't have anything planned for here; today was more about the stunning mountainous drive, rather than arriving to get stuck into activities. We go for a drive, intending to go for a walk and in the end, we decide to come back and have a little trip to the supermarket instead. *(Still no nail varnish remover for those avidly following this thread – my nails are looking a bit dire now – I've started the habit of picking them whilst daydreaming on the road, and keep having to hide the bits so I don't get in trouble for messing up the car.)*

I check my emails and have received one from a media company asking if they can use my dolphin video across their media platforms – how cool is that? You can watch this via my twitter account, @c_peache. I message them back to say I'm more than happy to for them to use it, so we will see what happens.

(Nothing happened with this in the end – well, not that I've seen. Not long after this email, the appalling Christchurch attacks happened and I'm sure the media were too busy in their coverage of this.)

Just another point on the rooms; sometimes when we first walk into them they smell a little musty. This is mainly due to them being temporary accommodation and not lived in all the time. I'm very sensitive to smells, and at first I can feel a little fed up about it and that we've chosen the wrong place. My advice; cook something; instantly this smell goes away and all is right in the world. It's not that the places are damp, it's generally because they might have been empty for a while.

As day 17 draws to a close I feel very privileged to be having this experience. I hope you're enjoying this journey with me and it's helping you to make some decisions about your trip; which is ultimately YOUR trip, and has to fit what suits you. But, so far I wouldn't change anything. We have been lucky with the weather, and for me that always plays a part in how your trip goes.

It's been nice having an afternoon in 'the house' faffing with our own stuff. I would advise adding this into your itinerary if you can. It's great to recharge the batteries and have some nice chill time to relax, and reflect on what you've seen and done. All the driving can make you weary, so handy to have the option of altering your plans slightly.

Accommodation: Last Resort Karamea – Karamea
Nights: 1
Number: 24
Type: Studio
Facilities: Fridge, microwave, toaster. A large sink! Again, no cooker. Overall very clean and tidy. Big spacious room. Large curtain to block out the light and people walking past.
Café/Pub: They have a nice café inside the main building with a bar
Price: £67.05

Wi-fi: Free and fast
Check-In: Fast, no problems
Parking: Right outside, plenty of spaces
Weather: About 15–19 degrees and cloudy, with drizzle throughout the day.
Skin colour: Nothing to report! I know, I'm as shocked as you!
Bites: None
Alcohol: Still nothing, not even a sniff of fizz.
Nail Varnish: And so the search continues...

Total Spent: *$55.87/£29*

P.S. We ended up having another look at our accommodation for Franz Josef. The reviews on second glance were not all that inviting and we did try and book places we could cancel in case our plans changed. The reviews, combined with the driving distances; having realised that's its true and all distances take much longer than on paper: we decide to split our journey from 2 nights in Franz Josef to 1 night in Franz Josef and 1 night in Haast. *(One of the best decisions we make.)*

Also, the likelihood of us doing loads of activities in the glacial region is slim. This might seem the wrong thing to say judging by all the marketing material, but reading reviews from people about the glacier, unless you can afford the all singing and all-dancing helicopter ride then it's a wall of dirty ice. I will confirm or deny this and whether we regret our decision to change our plans. If it's something I really wanted to do, then I would go for it, but I would rather see the glow worm caves in Te Anau to be honest, and this is all down to personal preference. It might be the main activity you want to do. We've read that Fox Glacier is easier to get to rather than Franz Josef Glacier – again we will see how this pans out.

Karamea to Greymouth
Day 18 | Thursday 7th March

The morning starts cloudy but warm, the sunrise over the mountains is beautiful yet again. The sun is trying to peek out past the clouds, ready to start the day. You can almost hear the sun saying, "Come on lads, get out of the way." Not sure why I decide clouds are male, but there you go.

A point on the beds… most have been comfy, but a few of them have had heated electric blankets on that have the hard control panel where you sleep! No, I don't understand it either. I advise you to check and whip these off before you attempt to slip yourself into bed. Unless of course you've come in a cold snap then I would guess you would rather be warm and cosy. I did contemplate putting them on to try and sweat away a few pounds but on reflection that's not a good idea. I always think electric blankets are scary, they lie there daring you to switch them on. Then during the night, they will slowly cook you; perhaps just my imagination.

We start the day with a cappuccino at the resort café, which is excellent, and the breakfast looks tasty; although we'd had breakfast in our apartment. For people worried about getting their daily caffeine fix, then never fear, all the local cafes we've been to have made excellent coffee; and if you struggle, there are McDonalds to fall back on. We mainly use McDonalds at home for the coffee, and obviously hangover food.

Car packed, butties made, we set off back down the mountain pass to make our way to Greymouth. Now I have to say, if I did it again, I wouldn't come to Karamea. I'm sure there is loads to do there if you want the outdoor activity side, but it isn't really for us, although we would have missed out on the forest path so maybe it was worth it. We did enjoy our chilled afternoon, so maybe scrap that. Again, it all depends what you want out of your holiday. Maybe the weather put a different slant on things as well.

Whilst journeying through the forest in the area of Mokihinui we come across a cheeky Weka! He/she is so nosey, and they obviously deserve the mischievous reputation they have. It comes right up to the car to have a look at us, and is trying to give the car a peck before we encourage it to move back into the safety of the forest. What an experience to meet one of these locals in the wild.

Next on the road is travelling along the Fox River on the West Coast. It's another must stop – the views of the beaches, crashing crystal blue waves against the rocks is jaw droppingly beautiful. There are loads of photo stop off points, and places you can break for lunch if you've brought your own. There are a couple of toilets stops along the way which is good. We stop at Westpoint to grab a drink and fuel up. It's a long way until the next petrol stop so worth getting some while you can. The fuel is more expensive in the South so far, but there's not much we can do about that.

The views of the Paparoa National Park are different to other areas, a lot more rock formations here rather than the sandy mountains we've seen so far. It's well worth a stop at the Punakaiki Blow Holes and Pancake Rocks. It's about a 20-minute slow walk around and free at the time we visit. Stunning rocks and crashing waves – it's windy though, so watch your hats! They have toilets here and a café, which serve a wide range of snacks, meals and drinks, as well as an information point about conservation in the area.

All in all, the drive today has been fantastic. From mountains to beach – what more could you want? The apartment has a proper stove – so we can cook! Chris makes a lovely veggie sausage pasta dish – tasty. We also have a sofa, the first one this trip – look after your sofa, you will never know how much you love it until you've lost it – that's not a top tip, just a general life statement. This apartment has a separate bedroom which is something new so far. It seems every place has positives and negatives, but we would go back and stay in all the places we've visited.

After checking in and unpacking, we brave a walk onto the beach which is about 3 minutes' walk from our room. The beach is large, stunning and full of rocks and driftwood with barely a soul in sight. The grey clouds are so low, with waves crashing on the beach, that there is no distinct separation between the land and the sky.

We've been trying to decide what to do re the glacier experience, it's so expensive, and I know it will be amazing as I've ready said, but I'm not sure it's something we're bothered about. For us, this is a road trip. I think we will see what happens when we get there. Cost vs desire is your constant companion during any trip if you have a budget.

A point to note. We are on the West Coast of the South Island. I say this now for your benefit. Stock up on a space suit, net, onesie and at least 42 gallons of insect spray. You will thank me later. This is the reason the bites have been listed since the beginning!

Accommodation: Greymouth Kiwi Holiday Park and Motels – Greymouth
Nights: 1
Number: 2
Type: One bed Apartment
Facilities: Large, it has a stove and a massive sink! Although the TV is a bit naff, it has a massive sofa. Always seems to be one thing that isn't good in these places. The Laundry room is next to room one and cost $2 for wash and $4 dry one load
Price: £78.24
Wi-fi: Free and fast

Check-In: Very quick, had a lovely chat with the lady about how you cannot get the staff nowadays and she was asking me what England was like as she'd always wanted to visit.

Parking: Free and right outside

Weather: Max about 20 degrees, been a beautiful warm day, started to get grey cloud and windy later on in Greymouth.

Skin colour: Tanned – result

Bites: None

Alcohol: Need you ask?

Nail Varnish Remover: You will see... *(Sorry total spoiler alert. I tell my aunty off for doing this with films!)*

Total Spent: *$151.47/£79*

Greymouth to Franz Josef
Day 19 | Friday 8th March

We have an interrupted night's sleep, due to the heavy rain. We both fell to sleep quickly but kept waking up and tuning into the sound of the rain before going back to sleep again. There is something quite comforting about it though; guess it reminds us of home. I find how we've slept is a daily conversation point during any holiday. Not that it changes anything other than maybe having to sneak in the odd siesta.

Wait just one minute now, before I go any further, I've got breaking news… sorry to spoil it and all that but I've found some nail varnish remover! I can hear a collective sigh of relief and also a small sadness inside you that this quest is now over. I found it in a New World Supermarket in Hokitika next to the cotton wool pads right at the end of the aisle. It's a shame that I picked most of it off yesterday in the car, but I will use it tonight and treat my nails to a shiny new paint job. I honestly don't know why it has been so hard to find!

On the subject of Hokitika if I had my time again, I would opt for staying here rather than Greymouth. Not that I have anything against Greymouth and the luxury of having a stove and sofa cannot be ignored. Hokitika has that little extra interesting vibe about it. Plenty to see and do and we treated ourselves to a wander, taking in the odd charity shop here and there. After this came the visit to New World supermarket which is where the nail polish remover was discovered. I'm pretty sure this was more exciting than any gold nugget discovered in a place called Ross; which is the gold mining area nearby. This is also worth a stop, and you can go panning for gold in *them there hills*.

The journey from Greymouth to Franz Josef is a real feast for the eyes – about 42 courses I would say. The tree-lined roads offer tantalising glimpses of the mountain peaks in the distance. The snow topped Mount Cook dazzles in the sunshine. There are a few stop off places near the lakes for a butty stop. We drive through places called Harihari, Whataroa, and Okarito – all stunning and worth a mention.

On the drive we reflect on the days of the week, trying to work out what day it is. This leads to a chat about the influence the days of the week have on you if you know what they are. At home, when working, most of us work to a timetable. Our work pattern is Monday – Friday, and I know some people for whom their Sunday is ruined because they have to get up for work on a Monday. Also, we have this new thing called Hump Day, on a Wednesday – a made-up day to make people annoyed and justify feeling fed up. That feeling when it gets to Friday – and then you have to enjoy yourself because it's the weekend even if you feel like being miserable. This is what a road trip is all about, discussions and putting the world to rights, and forgetting what day it is.

We arrive at Franz Josef and check into Glacier View Motel, which is next to the Tatare River, and we have definitely made the right choice to change our accommodation – not that we have stayed in the other one, but, this has better reviews and I can see why. Some places have that feeling about them. This is a little out of the centre if you want to walk into the main area, but they do offer a shuttle service. It's less than 10-minutes into Franz Josef by car.

After unpacking we head straight to the glacier as the weather conditions are perfect. It's approximately a 15–20 minute drive to the car park where you have a few routes you can choose from. It's roughly a 1 hour 30 minute walk to the glacier, so 3 hours return journey.

We opt for somewhere in between. It's roasting hot; how can it be so hot when walking to a glacier? I do not know. The walk itself is lovely, across glacial rivers and past stunning waterfalls. We take some beautiful pictures before heading back to cool down. Make sure you take plenty of water if it's a hot day. Another thing ticked off the list. We feel satisfied about our glacial visit. I wasn't sure if I would feel disappointed not doing the walk on it or the helicopter ride, but I don't. As with Hobbiton, if I really wanted to do it, then it would be to hell with the cost. The walk and the views were enough. I can highly recommend this, and it's free – music to a Yorkshire lass's ears! Although do pop some money in the donation box located on the way out if you can afford it.

Just outside this Motel is a weird collection of mushrooms and some lovely birds which I'm waiting to identify. Will update after the power of social media has looked them over. *(The birds were South Island tomtit; still not identified the mushrooms!)*

Right, time to get ready and meander into Franz Josef and see if we can get some food. Judging by the amount of people here, it might be a problem, as it's one of the busiest small tourist locations we've been to so far. The helicopters drone overhead constantly. They have been unable to fly due to the weather here, so they are keen to get the tourists up in the air.

Much later...

We have a nice meal in place called The Landings Restaurant and Bar on the main State Highway 6 road, and indulge in pizza and the biggest bowl of wedges we've seen – they beat us. *(The wedges not the staff – that would be rude.)* The meal and setting is lovely, the only problem... it's roasting hot! Honestly cannot get my head around the heat when there is a glacier in eyeshot.

We locate a pack of beer and a bottle of fizz before returning to the apartment. I would highly recommend staying in Glacier View Motel: the views are stunning, and the grounds are full of the little birds I mentioned earlier. We sit on some picnic benches enjoying our drinks and looking at the glacier – what an absolute treat.

We have 2GB free wi-fi/data with this accommodation. About halfway through watching a Netflix film we'd used it up – oops. I've uploaded a load of photos and checked some Instagram/Twitter stuff, but it seems to disappear pretty quickly. We both have about half of the data left we bought in Auckland. We've tried to only use the data when we have needed to. It's something to think about if you want to use your device; free wi-fi in your accommodation will save you a lot of money.

After another pretty fabulous day, something terrible has happened... I've lost the receipt with the nail varnish remover on! Can you believe it? After all that searching, in literally every shop we stopped off at... okay not every shop – more when I actually remembered to look. I think it was about $3.99. Anyway, my nails are nice and clean of silver nail polish for the first time in a long time.

Tomorrow we move onto the next property we changed only a few days ago; which is in Haast. Hopefully, another stunning journey.

Accommodation: Glacier View Motel – Franz Josef
Nights: 1
Number: 9
Type: Double Studio
Facilities: Another hot stove. This has the airiest feeling so far of all the apartments. Lovely outlook onto fields at the back and the glacier at the front as you would expect with the name of the hotel.
Price: £78.20
Wi-fi: 2GB free, fast but used this up very quickly.
Check-In: Swift and they gave us a map of the area and pointed out all the main places to visit. We were informed that the weather has been awful the past few days, so we have come at the right time.
Parking: Free and right outside
Weather: Raining as we left Greymouth, 12 degrees rising to approx. 6 million degrees as we walked to the glacier.

Skin colour: Still tanned
Bites: And so it begins... 3 for me, 16 million for Chris if the whingeing is anything to go by.
Alcohol: Back on the alcohol – yes!

Total Spent: *$105.41/£55*

Franz Josef to Haast
Day 20 | Saturday 9th March

It's a lovely start to the day with mist covering the ground and the clear view of the glaciers. I know I say this every day, but it's because we are up early enough to see it. We stop off at Fox Glacier, which is the baby to Franz Josef Glacier and enquire about some heli-flights they have advertised for $129, but they need a minimum of 4 people. Even with the extra food I've been eating we cannot make two people into four.

Thoughts of helicopter rides on our mind, we make our way to Lake Matheson and end up doing the full 4.4km walk around it. If you have the time, it's well worth a stop. It's like walking through an emerald forest except it has no yellow brick road. We spot a few of the local pigeons – a lot more colourful than ours back home. The lake creates fantastic reflections of the glacier in the distance, so take your camera. It's a cool shaded walk around the perimeter, with opportunities for any budding photographer. They have information boards which tell you about the trees and ferns in the area. A few moments into this walk, I take the opportunity to reflect on this amazing life-time trip. I'm truly grateful that I'm here.

(Sitting here at home, months after the event and editing this journal, I still have that same feeling. What a privilege it is to explore our beautiful planet.)

After this stunning walk we cannot resist the café and partake of some avocado, coconut and lime cheesecake – this is weirdly amazing. The first taste, you think – weird, and cannot quite place all the flavours – I don't think avocado is always the best flavour – but we haven't had much in the way of greens. Anyway, once the other flavours come through, it really is a taste sensation, and I highly recommend it. Let your taste buds catch up before you judge.

As we leave this idyllic location, the rear-view mirror provides constant glimpses of the glaciers which are playing hide and seek through the dense forests. We stop at a few of the lakes along the way to stretch our legs; there are so many, and I'm sure all of them are worth stopping at. Word of warning though, get yourself sprayed up against sand flies. The little shits are everywhere and bite without discrimination. We didn't encounter any of these in the North. We constantly feel itchy, like when someone mentions nits and you cannot stop scratching your hair – sorry this has probably made you itch now; but that's all part of the experience reading this guide, it takes you right there with us. I will warn you that I go on about the bites quite a bit, I make no apology for this. They are sent from the devil and the bites are painful.

Arriving into Haast, a small place, but it has everything you need.

> **TOP TIP:** *Fuel – if you have less than half then top her up whenever you get chance. Most petrol stations will say last one for 110 kilometres. But best to fill up and keep the tank full when you get the opportunity. Chris has used his card in a petrol station, and it took a $200 dollar holding amount which still hasn't come off 5 days later – something to keep your eye on if you have limited funds. He's using the WeSwap card. I don't know if that makes any difference as mine went back on a lot quicker using the Lyk card from Thomas Cook.*

I'm glad we decided to break up the journey. It's true that everywhere you go takes longer in New Zealand, for a few reasons: the roads are a maximum 100KPH, about 65 miles per hour; there are pesky tourists you have to sit behind; the views are so amazing you have to keep stopping and gawping, and why rush – you're on holiday! It all depends on how much you like driving and if you're sharing the driving, but a maximum of 3 hours seems to be enough. We like to set off before 9am so it gives us time to stop en route. We often arrive around 2.30pm and normal check in time seems to be 2pm. We then unpack and start part two of the day in whatever means we see fit. That's how we did it, you may of course do whatever the hell you like – it's your holiday.

After being tempted by Fox Glacier, we see a place offering heli-rides for $99. Being the tight gits that we are, we decide to check it out. That price obviously gets you about 2 minutes in the air. We strike a deal which costs us $550 for both of us. *(I know. I know!)* It's a 30-minute helicopter ride which takes us around the hanging lakes, following the glacier-fed Haast river, flying over rainforests, and landing next to a waterfall – sounds like our kind of trip. Seizing the moment and Chris's credit card, we seal the deal.

We have a couple of hours wait, as we have decided to go on the 5.30pm heli-ride. We have noodles for tea, now we have blown away most of the money we've saved since starting the holiday. We budgeted £100 a day not really knowing what the costs would be, and before the ride we were about £500 in credit on this. We are down to approximately £200 today after fuelling the car and the flight cost. But, for me the idea of being thrifty is to allow us to do something like this at a moment's notice and not worry we are overspending. Some folk will say, it's once in a lifetime, why not do it all; but any extra costs have to be paid when we get back and takes away from other holidays we like to have throughout the year. Also, we will try and have a cheap day tomorrow to get some pennies back in the pot. I have a feeling we might need more than £100 a day for Sydney, so I'm making sure we don't overspend here.

For those-eagle eyed amongst you, yes, we did have a stove top and after moaning that most of the accommodation doesn't have these facilities, we ended up going out for pizza. But it was Friday night, so what are you going to do?

So, that's it for now… about to get ready to tick another item off the bucket list…exciting.

Sometime later…

Well bloody hell, what an experience, if you are wondering about doing a heli-ride – stop wondering and just do it. I can 100% recommend the guys at Haast Scenic Flights @heliservices.NZ. The service and information were perfect. The flight over the Haast region – wow, there are no words.

The route we chose was The Hanging Lakes. The feeling of taking off and flying 3,000 feet above and through this stunning landscape is really the best experience in life. I want to re-train as a helicopter pilot now! To get to do this every day, it would never get boring as the landscape and weather changes with each day. I don't think I have the words to express how fantastic this is. There is only us and the pilot *(Obviously.)* on the trip and this makes all the difference as you get that personal touch.

We land near one of the lakes which is truly stunning and another experience to add to the list. There is a waterfall cascading down the mountainside and it is only easily accessible by air so it's a special experience. This whole area is part of the South Westland's World Heritage and I can see why. I always find any amazing life experience seem to go quickly, so getting to take off and land a few times adds that little something extra that we will never forget. It's worth every penny, and I encourage you to do it if your budget allows it. To be honest, driving through New Zealand is an experience in itself, all these other things are the icing on the cake, or the snow on the top of the mountain.

I can now answer the question, it was a good decision to change our plans last minute and incorporate some flexibility at the beginning of our trip by making sure our accommodation had as many free cancellations as possible. 100% yes, we never planned on staying here and I doubt we would have done the helicopter ride when simply passing through as part of our route. It would have been too late to do the heli-ride if we'd been en route to somewhere else. The time we chose was just right to catch a glimpse of the change of colour in the sky before sunset. We've been so lucky on the trip, the weather has been kind and we've hit the season just right.

We are now sitting watching the video footage we took on our phones and GoPro on the tv in the studio apartment. We pretty much held them up and hoped for the best as we were too busy looking at the sights. Hopefully, I can share them on my website. Once again New Zealand has been totally awesome.

One last thing before signing off on an epic day...

After the helicopter ride we went into the pub next door to where we caught the flight. It was like one of those moments in a film... we walked in and instantly wished we could walk back out. We were the odd ones out without our hunting gear on. Still we ploughed on to the bar. We are British; not known for making a scene. They did a glass of fizz so that's me happy. We ended up going outside even though we knew the flies were swarming, just waiting to drink some delicate foreign blood. It's very odd to be surrounded by all these hunting types, it's not something we encounter or is part of our circle of life back home. They are all friendly even if they are all packing hunting rifles somewhere...

Accommodation: Asure Aspiring Court Motel – Haast
Nights: 1
Number: 12
Type: Studio
Facilities: Microwave, stove, good facilities
Price: £85.42 – extra 2% cc charge
Wi-fi: 500mb free
Check-In: Quick and friendly
Parking: Free and outside
Weather: Started at 12 degrees and reached max 21, but felt warmer with the clear skies
Skin colour: Still tanned

Bites: Me 7, Chris– lost count – make sure you spray yourself when hitting the South – loads of people struggling today and getting bitten. Everywhere people were doing the fly arm dance. They are particularly bad here so please make sure you have some spray.

Total Spent: *Deep breath for this one... $677.15/£352*

(Yes I had to have a shot of Café Patron when I added it up as well.)

Haast to Wanaka
Day 21 | Sunday 10th March

We have a dodgy kip as the pillows are massive. Talking to the local guys in the apartment next to us in Haast who are on a fishing trip together, one wisely brings his own pillows with him. Even though it wasn't the best night's sleep, the place is quiet and spacious. It's nice chatting to the guys in the next apartment. They are born and bred New Zealanders, and one of them had visited Haast before the road bridge was built; crazy to think people were cut off until the 60's.

Also, I think the dodgy sleep might have been down to me being slightly paranoid about being bitten as there were loads of those pesky sand flies in the room, and even though the lights went off, and they went to sleep, that didn't help me to relax. I kept thinking I would wake up and my face and body would be one big red spot!

Please, please, please, make sure you bring some fly spray, blow torch, space suit, the sand flies are everywhere. I know I'm going on about it a bit, and I will bore you senseless, but there is good reason for it.

We've had an amazing time in Haast and it's time to hit the road, but first we start the day on a trip to Jackson Bay, as one of our new buddies next door, and the pilot, have suggested it's a beautiful place to visit. It's a long straight road to reach it: amazing how quickly you get used to the splendour of New Zealand and the stunning views, and a glorious tree lined road is the norm. As usual it takes longer than it should, mainly due to road conditions and road maintenance along the way at the time.

We arrive at Jackson Bay – wow, this is worthy of a visit, but we don't linger long due to… you guessed it; the pesky sand fly. You stand still and they are loitering around you with intent to bite within a nano second, and the bites smart a bit – not dangerous or so we have been told. I take my life into my hands using the toilet here. I'm convinced that I will have my backside bitten due to them hanging about constantly demanding that you them feed on your blood, but I think I managed it. Never been for a wee so quick!

The chaps from our apartment have followed us here and we stop and have a chat with one of them. He's one of those friendly guys who has an abundance of stories. If we weren't being eaten alive, we could have stood here all day. One story he did tell us was about the toilet in the bay – see it isn't just me that talks about toilets all the time! A fisherman who had 'something about him'… his words, said that he wanted Jackson Bay to be a modern area, and so he built the first toilet; put in a septic tank, the whole lot. On the day it was up and running, they had a grand opening and it was blocked within a few hours – or so the story goes. It's little gems like this that make a trip. He told us about cray fishing as a lad and shall we say borrowing some of the crayfish to eat. Honestly, I could have talked to him all day. Apparently, the crayfish could be plucked off the rocks in the early days before they became so commercial and their numbers have now dwindled.

He gives us some tips about visiting Milford Sound – we were going to visit via a bus trip but decided Chris will drive due to the stunning scenery, and if you get there before lunch you avoid the crowds of the bus trippers and those pesky tourists again.

> **TOP TIP:** *Anything you want to do, get there early to avoid any organised trips.*

We will see if it works *(It did.)* He also says that Doubtful Sound is worth a visit. A power station which was built to harness the water and you can drive through it? So, we might check that out. Local knowledge is better than the guidebooks. Well, apart from this guidebook of course!

(Sadly, after checking the internet, the power station is closed to visits and it's undergoing maintenance.) So, Milford Sound it is.

Leaving Jackson Bay and our new friend, we drive past the Haast river we flew over yesterday; wow again. What an experience to have. Something neither of us will forget. There is only one road to Jackson Bay, so you have to retrace your miles to get on the road for Wanaka. It's about two hours out of your way, but worth it if you have the time, and wearing a space suit. We are up early as normal so we arrive back into Haast by about 11ish, and then set off for Wanaka.

Right now, I'm sitting in our stunning apartment in Wanaka – it has actual stairs to a bedroom. When we planned our trip, we made sure that we slotted in a couple of better than average stays, just in case. Actually, most of the places we have stayed have been nice and clean. But this is a cut above, simply beautiful. I currently have the sliding patio doors open with a view onto a beautifully manicured garden overlooking the mountains surrounding Wanaka lake – I mean come on, that's living the dream. Chris is taking advantage of the quiet location, gentle breeze and having a snooze on the sofa. A road trip is about chilling and recharging as much as running around experiencing the place, and he does have to do all the driving.

> **TOP TIP**: *This place has a washing machine in the apartment. If you are away for a while I recommend you dot these facilities across your journey.*

Again, yet another stunning landscape to drive through. We've gone from the coastal roads to the mountain passes and now lakeview mountain passes. New Zealand really does keep the 'wows' coming – bit of a show-off really, lucky for us. Again, loads of places to stop off. Some nice waterfalls you can walk to within about a 5 minute walk of carpark. Three tour buses turn up, so we leg it smartish.

There is a nice coffee stop near Makarora. They do a fab cappuccino and banana muffin – but again watch the flies. Loads of places to stop; it's all up to where you prefer. Lots of people walking and cycling around this area.

There are stunning views surrounding the lakes around Wanaka, one being the Eely Point Recreation Reserve. There are places around this lake if you're heading here in a camper van where you can park for free – you couldn't ask for a better vista to wake up to. Wanaka is an upmarket and amazing place.

After finding out we have a hot plate, we head to the New World supermarket where lots of dazed tourists are wandering around looking confused about what to buy depending on their own cooking facilities. We make the most of the hob and Chris cooks us veggie burger and wait for it... wait for it... homemade chips! It's proper delish. We've also bought ingredients so we can have a proper veggie fry up tomorrow. Honestly, I cannot recommend this place highly enough. It costs £99 for one night; I would say on average we have been paying £65–£75 per night, and this is well worth the extra money, and if you can afford more than one night here, then go for it.

Wanaka has a posh feel to it, with lovely gift shops, coffee shops and bars. It reminds us of Windermere in the Lake District for anyone who has been there. The lake, mountains and general feel to the place are very much the same. We are staying in Queenstown tomorrow so we'll see how that compares. But, first impressions I would say stay in Wanaka and explore out from here. It's an hour's drive to Queenstown so easy to access if you want the hustle and bustle. I think I've gone over happy due to the experience yesterday and homemade chips!

The Golfcourse Road Chalets and Lodge is making us want to stay here and claim squatters' rights! Honestly, stay here and get room number 3. You will not be disappointed. I've discovered we have free Netflix in our room – this might be just a dream.

One strange thing, we were talking the other night (Back in the UK.) about New Zealand as we so often do now, and everything now gets compared to NZ. Anyway, we were talking about the homemade chips and the apartment and both of us said that we'd had a weird night's sleep, and both of us felt like there was some kind of presence in the apartment. But, we had not talked about this then. Maybe it was down to having stairs and an open apartment. Very strange that we both felt like this in such a safe place. Spooky.

Anyway, thus ends another day where this land keeps on giving, really cannot imagine how much more there is. I keep looking at Chris's bites and wonder if I can play dot to dot on them, but he probably wouldn't appreciate me doing that, and he did make me chips. If you look at our bites, they are a perfect dot to dot of our sock lines.

Me signing off after another fab day.

Accommodation: Golfcourse Road Chalets and Lodge – Wanaka
Nights: 1
Number: 3
Type: One-Bedroom Chalet
Facilities: Amazing, hob, microwave great facilities. All the facilities you could need. They have stairs! A luxury when you haven't 'gone' upstairs to bed for a while. Washing machine but no dryer, but they have a hanger dryer to put outside.
Price: £99.45
Wi-fi: Free
Check-In: Quick and easy
Parking: On site
Weather: About 14–21 degrees maximum temperature
Skin colour: Still tanned
Bites: Too many to count, I suggest you wear onesies to visit the west coast, or a bio hazard suit. You have been warned. Sand flies were created by the devil.

Total Spent: *$111.74/£58*

Wanaka to Queenstown
Day 22 | Monday 11th March

Wanaka is a lovely upmarket town as I've said, and if you can, I encourage you to add a few days here into your itinerary, you will not be disappointed. As with everywhere in NZ there is so much to see and do. But this place is on another level; it's so chilled and also it's nice to have a bit of a buzz with a few more people around, but not too many. As with all the places here, you could stay for three years and not do everything. Lovely bars and restaurants are dotted on the main front or grab a takeaway coffee and sit on the rocks drinking in the impressive views as well as your luscious cappuccino or your addiction of choice.

After breakfast and deciding it wouldn't be appropriate to try and claim squatters' rights, we sadly leave the apartment.

We drive around Lake Wanaka and stop off at a place called Diamond Lake. It's well worth doing the half hour walk around it. The lake is stunning, with the backdrop of the mountains, which is actually the standard backdrop around here. If you're lucky and it's a still day, the reflections make for a fabulous photo opportunity. The walk up and around gets the old heart racing but it's not too bad. There are loads of birds busy about their business. If you have the time, relax and listen to the sound of the birds; it's beautiful.

These walks every day have really invigorated our desire to start walking more when we get home. I broke my hip in 2012 doing the Yorkshire Three Peaks for charity. Yes that's 8 years ago – time goes way too quickly. Without boring you too much, it took over 8 months for the docs to discover I'd fractured it and by then it had healed – cleanly, thankfully. This took me at least 3–4 years to fully get over, due to this delay. By the time I was better Chris injured his ankle. Right pair of ailing duffers. Anyway, all these things have resulted in us not being able to do the walks we did in preparation for the Three Peaks Challenge, and we have hankered after getting back into them.

They say a trip like this changes you as a person. At the moment I don't feel changed, so much as re-invigorated with life. There have been so many changes on the cards for me in the past seven months, from accepting redundancy from my job as a Library Assistant in a College, to discovering a passion for writing and knocking out a couple of novels and novellas. This trip feels like a reset button has been tripped, and hopefully this will be the start of another bout of fitness and achievement. After all, why do we do this big 'life' trips, if not to be changed/learn from it somehow?

I've realised we are halfway through our whole trip and in 10 days we fly to Sydney. I feel like we need more time, maybe 5–10 years! I'm sure most people leave feeling like this. I have barely given Sydney a thought, which seems a bit rude, but with so much happening each day, it doesn't seem right to think so far ahead. I'm sure I can tune into it during the flight.

The road from Wanaka to Queenstown is better than we expected; the views typically are other worldly. You think it cannot get more epic and then it does. I don't know how anyone gets any work done around here. It's not a long drive, maybe just over an hour depending on how many times you want to stop to take pictures. We hit a traffic jam in Queenstown which doesn't slow us down and ends quickly, but still it was a jam – proof there are people in New Zealand.

We check into our stay at Garden Court Suites & Apartments, and then set off to explore what Queenstown has to offer.

When wandering around, I've come up with a foolproof way of seeing which direction tourists are travelling in around the island. Those with bites have come from the West Coast, those with legs fresh from red lumps are on their way. I feel like stopping them and warning them of the dangers. But that might seem a bit weird. *(When we go on a boat trip in Milford Sound I get talking to a few people and warn them about the sand flies, so hopefully I've saved a few people from the itching, burning and general discomfort.)*

Queenstown is a very cool place; the roads are in grid format to the main areas, which makes it easy to get about. Certainly, a lot more going off here. Every other shop seems to be an information/tourist shop, enticing you to book a sensational adrenaline adventure. We settle for wandering around and getting a cocktail, and very nice it is too. It's relaxing to meander around a busy city taking in the sights and smells. You won't struggle to find places to eat and drink here.

We eat out and end up having pizza again, which is very tasty. After this we walk a different way back to the apartment to see if we can avoid the hills, erm no. If you go down a hill you gotta go back up. Our route takes us past a pretty little church and to the waterside. Beautiful mountains reach the sea, ducks and grebes hang about doing their thing the same as they do at home. We come across a bench and find a camera someone has left. What to do? It's due to rain tonight so we don't want to leave it out. We end up leaving a note with my number under a rock on the bench, and to say we will drop it into the police station tomorrow, and hope that it will find its way back to the owner. We chill and watch the night close in on another day, waiting around for a little while longer just in case the camera owner comes back; but to no avail.

The next few days may offer some changeable weather so it may change our plans a bit, but we have four nights in

Te Anau coming up, so we are hoping the accommodation is good.

We have more or less a full day in Queenstown tomorrow, so we are going to make the most of it before our itinerary takes us to Te Anau. Pronounced T.R.New. Right now, it's dark and time to return to the apartment.

Accommodation: Garden Court Suites & Apartments – Queenstown
Nights: 1
Number: 341
Room Type: Standard room
Facilities: Microwave. Pleasantly surprised as most are studios here, but this room is huge and has full window/patio door to open to a couple of chairs. It's near the road so we will see how noisy it is tonight.
Price: £98.15
Wi-fi: Free and fast
Check-In: Fast and friendly
Parking: Free car park
Weather: Beautiful 17 – 22 degrees with cloud
Skin colour: Still tanned
Bites: Out of control, no new ones, but man alive in the night they were itchy! Little devils.

Total Spent: *$110.00/£57*

Queenstown to Te Anau
Day 23 | Tuesday 12th March

Before I add anything else, an update on the camera. We dropped the camera into the police station this morning. I left my email address as I was hoping it would find its way home.... And it did! So chuffed, the lady emailed me to say she'd been searching for it but couldn't quite remember where she'd left it. She was on the first leg of her world trip so I couldn't be happier that she has it back. She'd gone for one last look this morning and a chap mowing his grass told her about the note I'd left on the bench! Brilliant.

> **TOP TIP:** *I've now taken a photo which has my phone number and email address on in case we lose ours. Then someone can flick through our photos and be able to contact us.*

Anyway, back to today: we go for our standard morning coffee in Queenstown and stand on Marine Parade watching people go about their day. We are in one of 'those kind of moods' where we cannot decide what to do. In the end we go for the Skyline Gondolas, and this proves to be a good choice. I would call these cable cars rather than a gondola. The weather is supposed to be sending some rain, but this morning is glorious and the views from the top are spectacular.

We watch people jumping off the platform – bungee jumping. Something I've never fancied. I did a skydive last year with a friend for charity as I'd always wanted to do one – if you ever get the chance then go for it. Such a buzz. But Bungie jumping is not for me, thinking the snap back would probably re-snap my hip. The bloke that we just watched, looks like he will be suffering a nasty back injury despite his whoops. It looked like his body doubled at the wrong angle! There are a few gasps from the platform where we are watching it from.

After enjoying the views a little while longer, we go for a last wander around Queenstown. I love some of the road names here: Camp Street because my friend used to live on a street in the UK with the same name; Cow Lane – I'm not obsessed with cows or anything in case you were wondering.

Before long it's time to hit the road from Queenstown to Te Anau. As you would expect, it takes you through stunning landscapes. An area called Devils Pass is a winding road and reveals the crystal-clear lake hugging the roadside. Not for the first time we wish we were cruising on our motorbike. Nothing quite like a motorbike ride, but we cannot be picky.

After checking in, and breathing in the new carpet smell, we go for a reckie around the town centre, logging the coffee places and a quick trip to the supermarket to top up on essentials, like biscuits, alcohol and bread. The customer service is very good in NZ – you really feel like they are being genuine when they serve you and provide good service, it's a refreshing change. You have to go to Waitrose to get that in the UK from all the staff, in the other places it's hit and miss depending on the staff and the shop.

Like my home town of Newark-on-Trent in the UK, Te Anau has great amenities with shops, cafes, pubs, so you don't want for anything, but it's not busy like Queenstown. It's small but perfectly formed. Already I feel at home here and we have a fabulous apartment, and we know we're going to enjoy staying here. I love looking at road signs or maps and I find Quill St, Rodeo Drive, Snodgrass Road all being ones that stick in my mind.

The chap in Haast told us we made a good choice booking in Te Anau for four nights and he wasn't wrong.

This is our first 'long stay' at four nights, and it feels good to get everything spread out and know you don't have to pack up and leave by 10am which is the normal check-out time here. We've handled the moving about a lot better than I thought. I'd thought I would get fed up of it, but being organised with your bags and packing the car means it's really no bother at all. Maybe a longer trip will be on the cards in the future.

> **TOP TIP:** *On the subject of packing, we wondered what to bring as our plan was to do a road trip, and we wanted to make sure we could fit most of the stuff in the boot of the car. We have one medium size case and a carry-on sized suitcase and these fit perfectly in our Suzuki swift car boot along with our two rucksacks. We use a pushbike lock to secure them. To be honest it's not really needed as there doesn't seem to be much crime, but I feel better knowing they are locked up and out of sight in the boot when we park the car up to wander about a place en route to our next stop or stop to take pictures.*

We have less than 10 days left in NZ now, and it keeps popping in my mind that we will be leaving soon. I think there is a good chance we will back, somehow, one day. I wouldn't like to think I will never experience this place again. Then I tell myself to get a grip, we have 10 days left and most people only go on holiday for a week each year, if they are lucky! I know, I'm being spoilt and diva-ish but I don't care. I wonder what other delights this country will have to offer before we leave.

Oh, just a thought. If you get peckish on the road stop at any of the cafes, we've had some amazing muffins and scones. Today we stopped at Kingston and the cheese scone melted in my mouth. It looked like a boulder of a cake but was light as a fairy cake. I'm drooling thinking about it. These cafes are all along the roads, at around $4.50 $5.50

each, they are a bargain. I wish I could stuff my case with them. Only my mum makes better cakes. I best not start thinking about her cheesecake or treacle tart, else I will find myself on the first plane back to Yorkshire!

Tomorrow is forecast rain all day, but yesterday it said it would rain all morning and it didn't. I imagine it's hard to predict which way the weather will go with all the mountains. We quite fancy a visit to the Fjordlands Cinema in Te Anau as we watched a YouTube video about a guy that spends his life filming all the locations. The film called *'Ata Whenua Shadowland'* shows hourly at the cinema. The lady in the motel said she would give us a discount voucher, so that's a bonus. I also really want to do the Glow Worm caves, partly because it's my kind of thing; but also I've started writing a young adult story that has a glow worm cave and I think it will really help me visualise it when I come back to the story. This trip is about $98 dollars so that would be more or less our budget for the day for the both of us as we have £100, approximately $200. But we are nearly £300 in credit on spends despite the helicopter and various medical expenses.

Around this area is Milford Sound and this will be a must-visit. We are thinking Thursday or Friday when the weather looks better. On our trip around town we see a helicopter ride advertised... tempting, very temping. If any deals come along, I know we won't resist! I really want to save a little extra cash for Sydney though, as it's like London with the prices of activities. New Zealand seems quite sensible with most of its tourist prices. The gondola in Queenstown this morning was approximately £20, which seems good value.

As I type, I glance at the clock, it's 6.35pm and 25 degrees.

Right that's me done for the day. Once Chris has stopped snoring, we might go down to the lake to see if we can catch a sunset. I think we will be riding high on getting the camera back to the woman for a long time. I feel really happy to have helped someone out.

***

Much later...

The sunset is beautiful: we enjoy the view of the sun setting behind the mountain whilst enjoying a drink or two, watching the reflections change on the water as dusk settles. We are joined by two cats who start a face off and barely move. They are still at it when we leave. I get the feeling this is a nightly occurrence.

There doesn't seem to be many cats and dogs in New Zealand. I've read about Europeans introducing species native to the UK which have devasting effects on the other animal populations here. It's probably a good thing there isn't many, as a lot of Kiwis walk around barefoot, a testament to the cleanliness of the streets and I've seen no dog muck – probably due to the lack of dogs, but also people seem to respect their environment more. Not like the UK, if you walked about barefoot on our streets you be infected worse than a zombie in Walking Dead by the end of the street! There I go bashing my home country again – I love it really. The UK is a fantastic place with amazing places to visit; I think it has just lost its way a bit.

Many people walk along the lake and stop to take pictures of the sunset. We've been surprised by the amount of visitors from Asia here. You come across them standing motionless on street corners peering at their phones. Don't get me wrong, they are not the only ones. I partake of this modern activity. What is it about these phones that people struggle to look up, instead of down? They also seem to have to get a certain kind of shot. Last night in Queenstown I watched a few couples spend at least half an hour trying to get a selfie. For some reason the scarf had to be positioned in a certain way, and many adjustments were made. Just take the damn shot and then enjoy the view. They took the shot and then walked off, barely looking at the stunning landscape behind them. Might as well just photoshop themselves into the picture.

We comment on the fact we haven't seen many Maori in the South. Maybe we are not visiting the right areas, but it's a noticeable difference from the North.

Another day done...

Accommodation: Parklands Motel – Te Anau
Nights: 4
Number: 13 (Eek.)
Type: Double Room but more like a studio
Facilities: Has a double and single bed/sofa/table. Stunning apartment with loads of space and it's just been decorated as it has that new carpet smell. They have a fab shared kitchen facility with everything you could want. Laundry facilities available.
Price: £294.98
Wi-fi: Not very good. Used mobile data most of the time
Check-In: Fast and friendly
Parking: Right outside/free
Weather: Beautiful – hot here, approximately 24 degrees with cloud. The owner said it was warm for the time of year, and she was ready for cooler weather. Proof if you need any that NZ is like the UK.
Skin colour: Still tanned
Bites: Millions and itchy this morning, better as the day went on. But I'm a living, breathing dot to dot.

Total Spent: *$216.96/£113*

Te Anau
Day 24 | Wednesday 13th March

Another quiet evening. I will give New Zealand's it's due: all of the places we've stayed have been quiet. From the information I've read in the rooms, they don't tolerate noise, but we have woken to the promised rainy day. I don't think we've done badly to make it to day twenty-four before we've hit any noticeable bad weather. We had some in Karamea, and some overnight somewhere else, but that's it. Chris points out that it's the 13th of the 3rd and we're in room 13. Hope that doesn't bode ill!

After breakfast we make our way into town for a coffee and to check out the Fjordland Cinema. It has a relaxed feel about it and the cappuccinos are good. The accommodation gave us the 10% discount, so we book in for 7pm, the last showing of the evening to watch a compilation of the Fjordlands taken by helicopter. This is $20 so approximately £5 each.

The heavy rain is intermittent, and we're treated to a rainbow over Lake Te Anau and a little wink from Mother Nature to show she still has something up her sleeve. We decide to have a walk around one of the woodlands nearby. Today more than any other it feels like we're back in the UK. With the sounds and smells of the pine-filled forest and noise of the bracken underfoot, it's hard to believe we're in New Zealand, until you glimpse a never-ending mountain range in the distance that is. The wood is full of fly agaric mushrooms and we attempt some arty shots.

Standing on the edge of the lake with the rain bouncing off my umbrella, I feel very content. Walking through forests reminds me of my upbringing and 'leckin' in the woods was something me and my brothers did all the time with our mates. There is something magical about walking through a forest. You can see that it's turning to Autumn here, which is a strange concept when at home we are skipping towards Spring, but not until Barry, Larry and Sally or whatever they are calling the latest storm has finished with the UK.

After our pleasant walk, it's back to the apartment, and after lunch we spend a few hours chilling. Chris is reading his bike magazines and playing his game, and I'm writing this up and then finish reading the last few pages of my book; A Land of Two Halves by Joe Bennett – an enjoyable and informative read about a guy hitch hiking around NZ – well worth a read if you get the chance. Again, it's good to have a chill day, we have nowhere to go and nowhere to be, and it's nice. Everyone back home is asleep which still seems weird to me.

Te Anau is well worth an extended stay if you get the chance, a little like Wanaka, it's got that nice feel to it which is hard to manufacture. They really take care of their town. It has beautifully manicured hedgerows and stunning flowers edging all the gardens.

Days like these are made for reflection. Which means an opinionated ranting from me so feel free to skip to the next chapter. A time to press pause and think about the days I've experienced and the days ahead. My thoughts on New Zealand so far, well obviously its stunning, they are spoilt by the scenery. The towns are bigger than I thought, and nearly all are in the grid format, which suggest they've had the foresight to plan. Not like the UK, where history has designed our streets. Maybe the closest is Milton Keyes, which is a planned town. The people here are friendly and remind me of people in Ireland; the quaintness also reminds me of Ireland. It feels stuck in the past; a nice past, but that's not to say they don't live a modern life.

Well apart from one guy in Dunedin who will be extremely rude when Chris hesitates for a millisecond at a junction. You know earlier when I mentioned the swearing...

NZ is more religious than I thought. At the very beginning of my trip I said that I was sitting next to a girl on the bus from Auckland who told me that the country was 'very Christian' and I have to agree with her. There are a lot of churches everywhere, but I cannot say I've yet seen a person in one of them. I doubt religion will still be around in a few hundred years. I believe a lot of the conflict we're having nowadays is because it's dying out. People no longer need or want to be controlled by a 'God'. People want to live the modern life they see everyone else having. These things come with a generational shift; how many families go to church? How many kids are interested in religion? Maybe I just don't see it because I don't have many friends who are religious. I also don't believe you have to 'go somewhere' to show your faith. Or even have to have faith. Why can we not just be a nice human being? Each to their own though, if people want to believe and that gets them through life, then who am to say they are wrong?

The hunting element has surprised me about New Zealand. It seems embedded in their roots. In the shops there are magazines about pig hunting, deer hunting, and any other kind of hunting. I guess that comes with the outdoor lifestyle. The things people did in the past to capture deer for breeding for hunting is extraordinary. They literally jumped out of helicopters onto a stag! Madness. As I said after our heli-ride we went into a local pub and it was full of people in camouflage gear, the testosterone had to be waded through like a swamp. I don't understand the instinct to get a buzz out of needlessly killing animals. How can taking something's life, be a buzz? But it's their way of life. It easy to judge something that feels such an alien activity. I suppose, most hunt to eat the meat, and not just for sport.

Beer; a lot of the small shops don't sell alcohol, unlike every corner shop in the UK. I think there is some kind of law in NZ that if you drive past the 'booze shop' you HAVE to buy a box of beer... or maybe it's a distance thing, and it's prudent to pick up a box so you don't have to drive a four hour round trip to the shops. To be fair, I would be the same with Prosecco or Baileys.

I've said I like looking at street names as we are travelling the streets and highways, there something about seeing a familiar name when you're halfway around the world. Looking at the map of Te Anau I also see WetJacket Place. I wonder how this came to be?

I'm off to paint my nails now. I never got around to it the other day, and after having searched the length and breadth of New Zealand, I feel I have to use the nail polisher remover at least once more before I have to leave it behind. I might add it to a care package for the next person who decides to arrive with painted nails.

It's now 3.13, on the 13th of the 3rd in Apartment number 13. I take the decision to sit and wait for my nails to dry until at least 3.15 to avoid any problems.

Nails dry, we use the shared cooking facilities on site, which must be a first for us. This place is well-equipped and luckily no-one else is cooking at the same time. I know that makes us sound anti-social, but what if people tried to borrow some of our food! I mean come on, you can only take hospitality so far. Anyway, these facilities are a real bonus to this accommodation. The laundry room is next to this, so the site really has everything you could need.

Much later...

I can highly recommend the Fjordlands cinema. It's a cool venue to hang about in for a drink, and they have happy hour between 5.30–6.30pm with some free snacks at the bar. Not sure if this is every day. We watch the 30-minute film all about the Fjordlands area and the native species; when it was all discovered, and the impact of introducing non-native species. We both come away feeling inspired. What you see from your car or helicopter ride, your plane journey, skydive or paraglide is a fraction of what is lying behind these beautiful mountains. If this video tells us anything, it's that the land belongs to the land and long after us humans have become extinct like everything else, it will still be here in some way shape or form.

This land does not belong to the first people who claimed to inhabit it; it doesn't belong to the ones who came after to claim it. Us humans are as much introduced as the non-native species that have decimated the native species. Who brought these over you have to ask? The deer that decimated the fauna were introduced and then became a problem, the rabbits and stoats did the same. Maybe it's us humans that harm it as much as we harp on that we conserve and protect.

I did warn you that having too much time on my hands makes me think too much and go off on one. For your sake I hope you skipped to the next chapter!

Time for me to take my itchy legs and go to sleep, hoping that they calm down tomorrow and I can step down off my high horse. Actually, it's more likely to be a pony given my height. It could be the fizz that's doing it. I'm in catch 22. I need to drink to help my ailments, but the alcohol makes me waffle more – it's a fine balance!

Tomorrow we have booked a trip to the glow worm caves which I'm really looking forward to.

Total Spent: $99.25/£52

Te Anau Glow worm Caves
Day 25 | Thursday 14th March

After a very itchy night's sleep, I tell you those bloody sand flies are evil little sods. It doesn't help that I'm guaranteed to get these things worse than everyone else, although when we go into a local café aptly named 'Sandfly café' to get our morning fix, I spot a woman rubbing a liberal amount of a potion on her legs, 'guaranteed to give you relief'. So, I'm not alone. I see her face relax into a brief look of bliss as the itching subsides. I say to Chris that sand flies are small and deadly. He looks at me pointedly, obviously referencing that I'm not much over 5ft 1.5in. I shrug. When you're small it requires a bit of attitude to avoid being walked over.

We wait an age for our coffees. I would like to say its organised chaos but that doesn't really cover it. People queue in random places dithering over what to eat. I feel their pain as I need at least two cups of coffee in the morning to remember my own name. I hear my name being called past the wall of queuing people and make my way to get our coffees. I remember being in McDonalds in Greymouth and they'd run out of sugar! In most of the McDonalds they seem to give you a confused look when you ask for sugar; like you're asking for a sachet of salt… maybe the café culture is new here. They have none of the automatic coffee machines that are everywhere at home, and they make all the coffees by hand so to speak. If they did this in the UK, the cars would be queuing up for an eternity. Bet the tea drinkers have skimmed this bit... don't know a good addiction when they see one.

Coffee consumed we return to the room to use the facilities before visiting a bird conservation centre called Te Anau Bird Sanctuary. The plan had been to go for 9.30am as they feed the birds then, but we didn't wake up until 9.15 after our dodgy sleep, so never mind. We wonder if the maids will be in the room when we arrive back. It's a tricky thing to get right when staying in a hotel/motel, and a constant source of panic when we stay more than one night somewhere. Will they be in our room when we get back? If they are not there and they haven't been to service it, when are they going to turn up? Anxiety levels peak until they have finally done the deed.

***

We enjoy the visit to the Sanctuary. The place is free to enter, but as usual they have donation boxes dotted around – it's worth a few quid of anyone's money. Most of the birds have been injured at some point so are being looked after in total comfort from what I've seen. The flightless bird Takahe are interesting to watch – dinosaur throwbacks if ever I've seen any.

Before returning to the apartment after a trip to the supermarket for supplies, we reflect that we're actually missing being on the road. Staying in one place for a few days now has meant we've had the comfort and convenience of coming back to our room rather than moving on to the next place. Funny what you get used to. I thought I would struggle being on the road, but I miss it. This afternoon we're going on the glow worm trip and tomorrow is Milford Sound. This involves a two-hour trip, so it will be early to rise tomorrow. I'm very excited about both activities. We booked them at the information point in Te Anau and you get a discount if booked together.

Sometime later...

The glow worm caves are outstanding. It starts with a boat trip across Te Anau lake, which is the second largest lake in NZ and takes about 30-minutes to get to the caves.

We disembark and walk up to an area where 13 *(That number again.)* people have a guide who takes you through the caves, stopping at points to tell you about the history of them. It's a wonderful experience. The cave system is breathtaking, with large caverns and parts where you have to bend double to get through. Eels and fish can be seen when the guide lights the water. You arrive at a boat inside the caves and at this point you have to stay quiet. It's pitch black barring the light from the glow worms, if you look carefully you can see them swaying in the breeze. They look like tiny fairy lights lighting up the sky. It's an amazing trip which is well worth considering.

The different elements really make this a must do experience. I've never been on boat inside a cave before, truly magical and a little scary if I'm honest. At the time I was thinking, what if something happens to the guide? You could barely make out the shape of the person next to you. How would we get out? What if the zombies came and I haven't brought my emergency zombie bag along? You know how my imagination runs away with me, especially when left in the dark! If the character from my psychological thriller was in here I would definitely be terrified.

I've looked at some of the other glow worm caves, but I don't see how they could be better than this one. The cost is £50 each and it's well worth your time and money.

Another day sets on another experience. I cannot wait to visit Milford Sound tomorrow and hope the weather holds out for us. When tomorrow comes, we will only have one more week left in New Zealand. As with all holidays I cannot believe it's gone so fast, but when I think back to our first days in Singapore it seems months ago.

I know I will sleep well tonight.

Total Spent: *$282.74/£147*

Milford Sound
Day 26 | Friday 15th March

Early start for our epic trip to Milford Sound. We've booked the 11am boat trip and it's supposed to take 2 hours to get there, so we set off about 7.50am coffees in claws. I can recommend getting up early for this journey, if only for the sunrise. It creates the most beautiful sun-kissed mountains and adds to that the tree lined forests that hug the roads, the misty fields and low-lying cloud this morning are a real treat. At times, the sun dazzles through the gaps in the mountains. It's a chilly 3 degrees in some places.

Finally, we arrive at 'the tunnel': what an eerie experience this is; you travel down through the centre of the mountain with big water drips landing on the windscreen. Coming out, we're treated to more mountain ranges and general epicness that is a day in New Zealand.

We arrive in good time and park in the free car park. Making our way to the terminal building and after another coffee, we check in and get our boarding pass for the boat. We then sit, watching people scrabble to be the first ones on the boat.

Chris and I are transfixed by a bloke doing the most amazing stretches in full view of everyone. Now, I know it's a free country and all that, and the bloke is well within his rights to stretch; but why do it right in front of the windows? I want to look at boats and mountains and not his flexing buttocks. To escape the inner sights we head outside, as it's nearing the time of our boat trip. The pesky sand-flies are back! We are prepared though and spray ourselves liberally and hide every possible trace of skin. All around us people are doing the sand-fly dance trying to avoid them, some poor souls will realise their mistake in not being prepared when they start itching later. I'm tempted to go over and spray them, but they might not appreciate it.

On the boat…

We are treated to yet another good day of weather. We chose the nature scenic tour which takes two hours and fifteen minutes, and there is a guide on board who gives us loads of information about this UNESCO World Heritage area, and points out our lucky sighting of dolphins and some territorial seals; one of which does not want to give up his rock. Apparently, this is their way of practicing for when they go back to the main colony and they have to fight for their space.

Talking to a couple from America among the surprisingly sparse passengers on the boat, I warn them of the dangers as they will be retracing our steps. I chat to a few folk on the boat. It's nice to hear others' adventures and where they have been and where they are going. Sharing tips and insights is a great way to add something to your experience.

(I just looked this up for your information because I'm nice like that and I have a newfound hatred of sand-flies – it's the females that bite, they need protein for their eggs – cheeky bitches! Sorry, strong word and all that – but they bloody hurt.)

The dolphins are a delight to watch – when are they not? The backdrop of the fjords and cascading waterfalls make this a sublime boat trip which should not be missed. Lucky for us it's not windy today, so they take us a little bit further out into the Tasman Sea, and we spot an albatross flying low over the water. This is a must-do activity if you come to this area. They also have an underwater observatory which we were not aware of until we were on the boat. I would imagine that would be yet another fantastic experience.

> **TOP TIP:** *Book one of the morning trips as the bus trips haven't arrived. I would say there were less than 30 people on our boat. Go for the MV Sinbad, which is one of the smaller boats, they can get closer to the animals and waterfalls, and fewer people means everyone has room and it's easier to get them all important pictures. They also do free teas and coffees which is a bonus, and you can buy food on board.*

One of the passengers clearly has had a heavy night, or they are poorly, or they suffer seasickness and shouldn't be on a boat trip. At one point I'm seriously wondering if she is actually one of the living dead. I make sure I keep a closed door between me and her in case she kicks off and starts biting. Yes, I know I'm obsessed with Zombies and bites.

All in all, yet another great day in New Zealand. Tomorrow we move onto Dunedin and have our eye on a train journey along the coast. It's about the only mode of transport we haven't been on so far and turns out one of the most disappointing of our trips so far. We are going to try a bus trip further up the coast from Christchurch as we still haven't given up on seeing penguins and whales, although it seems it's around the December time when you can catch a glimpse of these fabulous animals. *(We never manage this boat trip due to running out of time.)*

Te Anau has been a great place to stay. It has everything you need from Supermarkets, coffee shops and bars. This site is great, it's quiet and about a 5-minute walk into the town centre and about the same to the lake side. They have cute kittens hanging about the complex as well, although by the time you read this they will have grown.

On the food front, you really can eat cheaply. We had a pumpkin and feta lasagne from the fresh section in the Freshchoice supermarket – $5.99 – absolute bargain and really tasty. I'm dreading adding up what we have spent on coffees though – it will lay our addiction bare for all the world to see. Might call this a coffee guide to New Zealand.

Some very sad news…

I've just seen on the news that there have been some potentially fatal shootings in a Mosque in Christchurch, our next stop in a few days' time. So sad, that these things are still going on. Honestly, is this the best way that people can express their views? So incredibly sad for the people who have been injured. Having travelled around New Zealand you realise no matter how vast some areas are, it's also like a small town where everyone knows everyone, or of them, which means today will affect a lot of people. It's something you sadly expect of America almost weekly, and thankfully only occasionally the UK; although still more than it should. But, quite shocking that it's happened in Christchurch.

Total Spent: *$289.90/£151*

Te Anau to Dunedin
Day 27 | Saturday 16th March

A strange sleep, and a strange morning to wake up in New Zealand. Last night I spent a few hours watching the news unfold on the tragedy in Christchurch: at the time of writing this they believe 49 people have died and many injured, in one of the worst massacres in New Zealand's recent history. A man went into Mosques and shot people. I won't go into any more detail, it's all on the internet, and I believe these people do it to get some kind of weird fame out of it.

It feels odd that we will be heading to this city in a few days. What will it be like? How will the people cope with this tragedy? Will it change the feel of the city? I feel sad not only for the people affected, but also, maybe selfishly that this has happened while we are here. New Zealand is known throughout the world as a safe place. I still believe it is, there is nothing even the best countries' security can do if someone wants to do something like this. Nothing. I'm sure the blame will start, but some people are evil and do evil things.

Sadly, we have experienced this in the UK on a few occasions. We visited London a week after one of the awful atrocities and, to be honest, it didn't feel any different. People will be people and get on with their normal lives. I believe you have to get on and not let these things change your plans; to me, these people have won if you change your life because of them. It doesn't mean you're not respectful or saddened by events, it is just two fingers up at these evil people who try to affect your life.

Anyway, I felt I needed to put down my thoughts on this. My heart goes out to the people and to New Zealand.

We leave our four day stay at Te Anau, and very pleasant it was; again some lovely experiences that will always stay with us. We grab a coffee from the Sandfly café; great coffee. We didn't eat here, but I think everyone in Te Anau is having breakfast here this morning. The food looks great and the staff are friendly and efficient, even if the visitors seem not to know where to stand.

The road from Te Anau to Dunedin changes from the mountains to rolling fields full of sheep and cattle grazing under the clouds. Some of the towns are big; something that has surprised us. Some are not in the guidebooks I've read but are larger than the ones advertised. Maybe they want to keep some of them tourist-free, so they have peace and quiet to go about their normal day. We stop off in one of the towns so I can fulfil my coffee addiction and, I kid you not, everyone turned to look at me! Friendly looks, not like something out of a horror movie, but still it makes me chuckle. Maybe it's the events at Christchurch has naturally made everyone on edge.

Driving here we took our usual guesses on the satnav kilometres. The reason for the title of this book, you set the directions on the satnav and it basically says, 'In 187 Kilometres, turn left!' I guess at 85 kilometres and Chris 150, when it comes up, it's 149 kilometres, I'm sure he's cheated and checked earlier; not that I'm a sore loser!

After checking into Leith Valley Holiday Park and Motels our accommodation for the next two nights, we walk into the city? Town? For a wander. Dunedin has Scottish heritage/history, and you can see it in the surrounding brick buildings. This is a University town, and adds a 'youthful and generally pissed' population from what I've seen today, and it has plenty of drinking holes to accommodate them.

It feels really odd coming into such a vibrant place. We almost feel like turning around and heading for the hills. Amazing how quickly you adjust to the lack of people. This is where everyone is; all gathered in Dunedin. I wonder if there are some people who never leave these places due to the distances and time to get anywhere.

We tuck into a pre-prepared curry from our favourite supermarket, Countdown. Yes, even though we have a stove top! First thing we will do when we get home is to make a Sunday roast – even if it's hot.

On the journey to Dunedin we started talking about home more. We are coming to the end of our holiday in New Zealand; this experience that was a few years in the planning. All those ideas of what it would be like, would everything go to plan? What would we see? All these thoughts and plans will soon be coming to an end. It's our way of getting ready for it. Even though we still have 5 days left *(Oh my God, 5 days – I thought it was a week!)* in New Zealand, and then the amazing experience of a week in Sydney, and a two day stopover in sweltering, sweaty, humid heat of Singapore to look forward to.

Indian eaten at lightning speed, we go to explore the river that is right behind the apartment. An old bridge leads us into an area that used to be quarried, and this site is where an old papermill used to sit. It's very eerie walking through the low slung branches all covered in moss and lichen, the river a constant source of noise, covering up the footsteps that fall in step with your own – okay I got carried away there – made me come up with an idea for a spooky story; that's how atmospheric the place is. There are also glow worms hanging off the rocks near here, but you have to go in the dark to see them – yeah right and get killed by the serial killer who clearly lives in the forest – I'm not daft!

This site is really interesting, and we have views of the green hillside and the death serial killer valley. *(It's obviously not really called that!)* So far, it's very peaceful, as they have all been.

(Today we have had to email the company from WeSwap as the petrol amount still hasn't cleared onto Chris's card. Updating this now back at home 3 months later, the money never went off the card, so no idea what happened with that transaction for fuel.)

Accommodation: Leith Valley Holiday Park and Motels – Dunedin
Nights: 2
Number: 2
Type: Superior One-Bedroom Apartment
Facilities: Stove hob, microwave – nice large apartment. Room right next to the reception area. Free milk on the first night.
Price: £144.00
Wi-fi: Free and fast
Check-In: Fast, friendly
Parking: Right outside/free
Weather: Cloudy, overcast and then bright blue skies 14–19 degrees
Skin colour: Still tanned
Bites: No itchiness, just bruising

Total Spent: *$58.90/£31*

Dunedin
Day 28 | Sunday 17th March

Well, again it was a weird old sleep last night. All night I was thinking about what happened in Christchurch and what the families are going through, maybe the fact we are going there tomorrow makes it hit home all the more.

***

Leith Valley is a lovely site for anyone wanting to stay. Only about a 30–40 minute walk to the train station where we do the scenic seaside trip on the train. Out of all the things we've done, this was a bit, well, crap. It does follow the coast the whole way, but sadly if you're on the left hand side of the train you get to have a lovely tour of the rocks and trees that face the sheer rock on the way, the highlight being the odd cone or sheep to break up the view. The views on the right side are much better, although the commentary is like this… someoneCreatingAHashtagAndBasicallyAllOneWordMeldedIntoOneSoYouHaveNoIdeaWhatTheHellHesTalkingAbout.

I must say even though it wasn't the best experience, we like to make the best of it so we try to get excited when there was a break in the gaps of the trees… perhaps we have heat stroke or something. We spot a cone loitering with intent at the side of the banking and wonder if he and his friends are plotting to shut down a road...

(I must admit to having a break from this, and not writing any more today. This is the first time on the trip that I haven't written up the day's events. To be honest I just didn't feel like it. I think the events of Christchurch have affected me; well both of us.)

Added the next day...

To follow on a bit from my earlier post. On the train journey, many of the sights cannot be seen from the road; this is because most of them are boring. I know I'm doing this a little disservice, but it wasn't what we expected and out of all the trips it's the one I wouldn't do again. Although it was interesting listening to the people from the cruise ship. It was like a game of Top Trump Cruises. Each person was trying to outdo each other with which cruise they had been on; where they had been. 'You should have visited so and so when you went there.' 'Oh we did this.' 'It was better if you did it this way...' My w....' Sorry won't carry on with that. I get the feeling that some of the people are only cruising to show off, rather than for the experience.

On this subject, I will not lay myself open to any prejudices, but I will say that while we were waiting for the train to come, one enthusiastic photographer decided that it would be a great idea to get on the tracks! Yes, you heard this correctly! I will leave it to your experience to fill in which nationality this person is. But generally, they seem to take more pleasure out of spending 3 hours getting a photo of themselves rather than enjoying where they are. Now don't get me wrong, I had to buy extra Cloud storage as I've taken that many pictures and videos; but I like to think I also absorb the experience. If I miss out on a picture for an experience, then so be it.

After our disappointing train journey, we spend the rest of the day wandering around Dunedin where we see a lot of very drunk students at 9am in the morning and it reminds me of my youth. They're all dressed up for St

Patrick's Day and the green students make it look like an incredible hulk convention. I'm quite shocked by the mess and destruction we see. I hope this is just one of those crazy mad weekends because so far NZ has been very clean and tidy. A lot of the streets that obviously have students living in them are very messy with lots of smashed bottles and rubbish outside the houses.

We head into the centre and have a drink and some food, but I'm really not feeling the vibe of Dunedin. Maybe it's me and the circumstances, but out of all the places I wouldn't visit here again, or maybe visit a different weekend as I'm sure it has more to offer.

Total Spent: *$228.31/£119*

Dunedin to Christchurch
Day 29 | Monday 18th March

It's a long drive from Dunedin to Christchurch, but very scenic, so much better than the train journey. Because of the mountains, we go from misty, dull, atmospheric and then drive into pure sunshine and our feelings change according to the scene and the weather.

We stop at the Moeraki boulders, and there are many tourists standing on a boulder ruining the chance of anyone getting a picture without having to photoshop them out of it. We snigger as people look very annoyed. There are so many tripods set up it looks like something out of the War of the Worlds if you squint down the beach. I wonder what pictures they are trying to get. Yes, the boulders are interesting, but do they warrant that much filming? Maybe they have to film them all day to get a picture without someone standing on them. I scoff a scone from the café and angle my camera to get a few pics without people in, sure in the knowledge that I will probably only look at these once when I get home; which begs the question why do we take so many pictures of everything?

After leaving here to continue our journey we stop in a strange and wonderful place called Oamaru. It's home to a steam punk museum and lots of weird and wonderful buildings and art structures. Definitely worth a stop off. Wish we could have spent longer wandering around, but the road is always calling.

The Littlest Hobo lyrics are in my head right now…

I admit to feeling apprehensive about coming to Christchurch. The whole atmosphere naturally changes after a disaster, even if people do carry on with their lives.

We arrive into the South Brighton Area and after checking into our little cabin *(More about this later.)* we go for a drive into the nearest town as it's heading for dusk.

I'm surrounded by campers which naturally makes me anxious due to my real hatred of camping. The cabin is something you would expect to find in the Alps with a real roaring fire and furs; but this has no fire and no fake furs and extremely basic facilities. For both of us it brings back memories of childhood holidays, which is something I believe we all try to recreate as adults. But even back in the day they were better quality than this cabin.

Chris initially feels a bit disappointed with central South Brighton. It's bit like a neglected seaside place that's left its heyday in the past. But, we have arrived after a long drive, so we will see what it's like in the bright lights of the blue sky and sunshine tomorrow.

We decide to drive into Christchurch for our normal Countdown visit for supplies. This experience is very poignant. Is that the right word? By total accident, mainly because Christchurch isn't a big place, we drive past both of the streets with the Mosques where the terrible tragedies happened. We also drive past the main area where people are gathering for a vigil; lots of people making their way to the area with flowers. The amount of media there is shocking. It hits home all the more that something very bad happened in this wonderful place.

It almost seems crass to be thinking about doing 'holiday' type events when this has just happened, but as I've said we have to carry on, because we feel that not only is it two fingers to the people that are trying to change people's lives, but also humans are fabulous at processing terrible events and dealing with them and moving on. It doesn't mean you have any less compassion for the people, city, country, and world it's affected. If I'm being honest, you also feel relieved it hasn't personally affected you in terms of someone you know. A normal human reaction, even if many won't admit it.

I feel like I shouldn't make this about the event, but how can I not? It's the last few days of our time in New Zealand and I'm sad for them and us that this is where we end it, because I'm sure Christchurch has so much to offer, but the poor buggers have been dealt a blow. We feel like we shouldn't go in and do the touristy things, but at the same time surely spending money and enjoying ourselves is a positive, supportive thing to do at this time. I suspect neither would feel right. It is possibly the only time we will visit New Zealand, so will act accordingly, with our thoughts and feeling resting with the people affected.

Tomorrow is the start of our last days in the stunning, wonderful and special place that is New Zealand. We will enjoy this beautiful place and the memories it has to offer and keep us into our old age. We will enjoy what it wants to show us and embrace being visitors to this place that is on the other side of the world from the UK but feels so much like home.

Accommodation: South Brighton Holiday Park – Christchurch
Nights: 4
Number: T1
Type: Studio
Facilities: Portable hob, kitchenette. Microwave. Bit tired, smells of wee, but cheap.
Price: £226.00
Wi-fi: Free and not bad, 1GB each day
Check-In: Quick and friendly
Parking: Right outside/free
Weather: Overcast, but really warm when sun came through the cloud
Skin colour: Still tanned
Bites: No itchiness, still the bruising. Hurrah

Total Spent: *$198.53/£103*

Christchurch
Day 30 | Tuesday 19th March

Well after a bit of a rough night, this seems the standard way for each day to start. I confess to having a few days of feeling tired, but what can you do but get on with it? There is an aroma of, what shall we say… urine to be polite, coming from the bathroom. The accommodation we are staying in is a log cabin as I've said, which means they can be a little bit like a caravan when you first inhabit them. If they are closed for a while, they are a bit fusty. I also suspect that the place has never had a full deep clean.

We do the usual Brit thing and wonder if we should complain about it. Cracking open the curtains we find a cloudy but nice day and decide to go out for our normal coffee run and think about complaining about the accommodation. Not having been impressed with the South Brighton area last night, we travel a little further and discover a fantastic place called Lyttelton and find a café overlooking the port area.

Lyttelton is what I would call, very shabby chic, having been hit hard by the earthquake and it's clear they are still in the process of rebuilding this area. Art galleries, cafés and gift shops with locally made produce are dotted along the main high street, giving it a Camden feel to it. Apparently, they have co-operative projects going on here in which the residents get to invest in projects, which is as it should be and must create a lovely community. This has a nice feel to it and is well worth a visit and we will be regular visitors whilst in this area.

Coffee done, we carry on around this peninsula, and I'm so glad we do. If you're in this area and you have a car, then go for it, you will not be disappointed. Our first point of call is Corsair Bay Reserve. We are lucky enough to spot a kingfisher hanging around on the rocks and we stand for a while watching loads of little birds go about their daily business. It would be very easy to relax here all day and watch the world and the wildlife go by. There are some lovely headland walks around the area.

Changing our plans from the activities in Christchurch, we return to our shabby shit cabin and knock up butties to take with us, including our standard ginger beer – the Famous Five would be proud.

Next stop on the road is Allandale Reserve. For the bird watchers, you will enjoy this place, there are so many different varieties. Little crabs hide in the thousands of holes that cover the beach. Simply beautiful.

We stop at a little place for coffee – of course. The food and cakes look amazing, but I'm denied these little pleasures by Chris. Although it's probably a good job since it's day 30 of our holiday and I cannot keep using 'I'm on holiday' excuse to have 'treats'. They might refuse me a place on the plane if they pop me on the scales. We had to get weighed when we did the heli-ride in Haast – I didn't even get chance to go for my pre-weigh-in wee, which I always did when I attended Weightwatchers many years ago.

This coastline really is stunning, and, like most places in New Zealand, thankfully lacking in people. It's so peaceful: the only sound is the lapping of the gentle waves and the odd bird making its presence known. It does not get better than this. There have been many wonderful experiences on this trip, but by far for us is cruising in the car, taking in the sights and stopping off to explore beaches and towns.

Happy and content with our wonderful drive we take a cruise into Christchurch after dinner, but the vibes of the city are still with us. It's a sombre feel, with too many media vans jockeying for space, where there should be a peaceful park for locals and visitors to enjoy. We find a bar for a drink where laughter and friendship are in the air.

People are still here, having fun and carrying on with their way of life. I doubt the tragic events are very far from anyone's minds, but we humans have that capacity to decompartmentalise our feelings, and it's a bloody good job!

Day set and done. Looking forward to getting out and exploring tomorrow.

Total Spent: $125.28/£65

Christchurch

Day 31 | Wednesday 20th March

Today we decide to visit the Wildlife Park in Christchurch called Willowbank. I'm always a bit dubious about visiting a zoo/wildlife parks and like to make sure they are about conservation, and not just an attraction. We want to see a native Kiwi and visiting here is pretty much the only way. Generally, I would rather see animals/birds in the wild, but I think Kiwis need to be left alone – they don't want a load of humans gawping at them while they're trying to get on with their normal life. In the wildlife park they have an enclosure which mimics their forest night-time foraging environment. It takes a little while for your eyes to adjust, but when they do it's such a treat.

We visit the enclosure a couple of times, and spend some quiet time watching them go about their nightly endeavours. Their beaks are well suited to digging the ground to find their evening feast – maybe that classes as breakfast for them. They are a delight to watch and it's quite obvious why they don't fair well against predators – they are basically, a big body with feet and a large beak, which don't look adjusted to survival in the wild.

There are so many animals, birds, fish and creatures to enjoy watching going about their daily lives in the park. We spend about four hours here, which is pretty much a record for us. You can feed the eels; which is really interesting to watch. They also have lots of extra feeding times to get closer to the animals. Some you have to pay for; which all helps the park to pay for looking after some of these wonderful creatures. There is a charge to get into the Wildlife Park, but it all goes towards conservation.

The pigs are a particular favourite of ours, and the baby piglet; well, I say baby, it's massive, but not quite the bulk of its parents just yet. As soon as we stretch out our hands it's on its side basking in the bliss of a belly rub.

The centre mainly has volunteers and has a medical facility where sick and injured animals are brought hopefully to be fixed and set free. They also have a breeding programme for the precious Kiwi. All in all, a fab place to visit and one to put on your list.

We naturally indulge in coffee and cake whilst there, and highly recommended you do the same. All the food looks delicious and I sigh again thinking of the damage I've done to the waistline. We excuse the cake by once again stating, 'We are on holiday' and, yes, for people who are reading this who know us, believe, that we are constantly on holiday. I haven't got the nickname Judith for nothing. But when you choose not to have children, life is a constant holiday. At the park you could see it written on the parents' faces – they wonder why they paid to come in when their kid is playing on a knackered old tractor and has no interest in the animals on display, or screaming to go home.

After this very pleasant visit, we head back to La Shabby Shack. To be honest, we are tired after walking around for most of the time we were in the park, so, it's nice to chill out and relax. I update my journal, while Chris downloads the GoPro videos. The site here is so quiet and chilled, and it's a shame that the unit lets it down – although the accommodation is cheap. I reckon a good deep clean with a liberal amount of bleach and about £100 spent on the décor would make it of high quality. That seems indicative of most of the places we have stayed at though. I wonder if they work to such a tight budget, they cannot afford to maintain them. Or maybe they don't have the time. Some of these sites must require a lot of looking after with most guests only staying one or two nights. This place was maybe the cheapest out of the lot when we were sitting in a pub in London booking the accommodation after the excitement of finally booking our flights. We would stay here again as the site is well catered for and in a good location, but maybe in a different cabin or ask for the place to be properly cleaned first.

Again, thoughts go to our leaving New Zealand in a few days. I mentally run through the list of things we have purchased since we barely had any space in our cases as it was. Unusually for us, we haven't worn everything we've packed. We are used to travelling light. Having had motorbike holidays in the past, you get used to travelling on the lighter side. I think the novelty of checking in bags has made us get carried away. Chris has bought so many pairs of shorts, he could change three times a day! I've brought a few dresses, but have been more comfortable in leggings and a top. Also, I didn't want to get put into quarantine if any health officials see the horrific sand fly bites on my ankles.

Amongst everything else Christchurch has now had an outbreak of measles. The last thing I want is to be spotted in a dress with my bites on show, I will be in quarantine quicker than Elliott from E.T! This country doesn't seem to be getting a break at the moment.

After a lazy afternoon we follow the sat nav to the Banks Peninsula. This takes us through a place called Little River – which is a nice stop with some weird looking silos which you can stay in. They have toilets, cafes and shops to peruse. There are a few interesting areas to visit en route; the Birdling Flats being one of them, which apparently have gems and fossils – *not something we get chance to look at.* Arriving in Akaroa, the views are once again breath-taking. This place is a fantastic area to visit – a very French feel to is due to its past history, well worth looking up and visiting.

We spend a very pleasant hour chilling in the most fabulous bar overlooking the sea, with the setting sun glinting on the water. Stunning. We keep our eyes peeled for whales as we've overheard someone say they are seen in the bay.

The road to this area is tricky if you're not a confident driver, mountain passes, switchback roads, sharp turns, with mountain views, clouds dancing across the mountain tops creating shapes on the green fields. Chris is in his element.

If we thought the drive here was amazing, it's nothing to the drive back. The sunset is sublime, the sun kissed mountains and green water glinting below making me want to rip up my passport and refuse to leave. It's difficult to put these feeling into words. If you could bottle the feelings and let people see it through your eyes it still wouldn't convey the beauty. Just when we think New Zealand can offer no more, it offers up a little smirk and gives you a sunset delight followed by a Super Moon on arrival back at our accommodation.

Tonight, we go to bed very grateful, and happy for these amazing experiences.

Total Spent: $157.67/£82

Last full day in NZ
Day 32 | Thursday 21st March

Another day, and another set of feelings. Our last full day exploring this beautiful country. We still haven't explored the main area of Christchurch, so make for the centre. Having driven through a few times, we haven't really got an idea of what there is to do. Obviously, the terrible earthquake has certainly left the place with a lot of rebuilding work. People seem edgy as well, and naturally so.

I don't know what it is; maybe last day grumpiness, the feeling that we need to have a good time in Christchurch… but it really isn't doing it for us. These things are creating the perfect storm which allow the threads of discontent to unravel. It's easy to take it out on each other, but having put up with each other for 20 years we recognise the signs, and decide that it isn't going to be our time for Christchurch on this trip, and there is no point forcing it.

The area's that look like they would be the tourist hotspots were hit heavily in the earthquakes in 2011. I remember hearing about this on the news. As with all of these things, you feel for people but it's not on your doorstep, so your thoughts naturally turn to things to home. Also, it was 9 years ago, and honestly, I thought that would be long enough to fix it, but it's clear it's more complicated than that. They have maybe taken the opportunity to rethink and rebuild areas. There is a lot of construction going on. Also, I'm sure they want to restore things sympathetically, and that takes time.

We cut our losses and find a coffee shop. *(Naturally.)* We then regroup and decide to return to the apartment to do a pre-pack check and then return to the Banks Peninsula, since road trips and views are really what we came for.

It doesn't disappoint. Further round the bay is another area with some lovely tourist shops to peruse. If you can add this amazing place to your itinerary then do so, if you can afford to stay here then you will not be disappointed. So, so beautiful. We partake of some fish and chips from Murphy's on the corner chippy in Akaroa– wow – delish. Go on treat yourself. Word of warning; the chip portions are massive.

Having explored a lot of New Zealand, but perhaps only the tip of the glacier, I can say that I can 100% see why people compare this amazing country with the UK. I've been lucky enough to visit a lot of places in the UK, and can see elements from every part: the epic mountains of Scotland, the Lake District, Peak District and Yorkshire Dales; the flats of agricultural Lincolnshire, the wooded areas in Wales; stunning coastlines including Devon and Cornwall and quaint places like the Cotswolds and Surrey. The industrial/historical areas of the towns are like home. You could be driving through my hometown of Newark on Trent, Derby, Wakefield or any one of the towns and cities in the UK.

The only comparisons you cannot make is to places like York, London, Leeds or any other major city, mainly because there aren't enough people in NZ to make up the hustle and bustle of these places and they simply do not have the history we have. Maybe the nearest I felt to this was in Auckland and Dunedin. New Zealand is still a baby in terms of history if comparing it to the UK. Just as it's a treat to see New Zealand in its raw beauty, mostly untouched by humans, they must be in awe of the history and the sheer amount of people in the UK towns and cities. New Zealand is slightly bigger than the UK in mass, and the lack of people is a real gift to this land, and I can see why they control the numbers.

One very important thing to note out here: the Crunchie bars are so much bigger than the UK! Honestly, don't know what has happened in the UK, but ours get smaller every day. In New Zealand they are the size of the remote control. I will take this up with someone when I get home, a strongly worded letter needs to be written. Probably get blamed on Brexit like everything else.

Our last full day... done.

Total Spent: *$54.50/£28*

Leaving New Zealand
Day 33 | Friday 22nd March

Nooooooooooooooooooooooooooooooooooooooooooo
oooooooooooooooooooooooooooooooooooooooooooo
ooooooooooooooooooooooooooooooooooooooo...
Can I do a whole chapter with just NO? I once listened to an audio book which had the work 'fuck' used throughout one whole chapter; I think it was 'How to be a Vigilante' by Luke Smitherd. I quite like the idea if this was an audio book that the narrator says, 'Nooooooooooooooooooooooooooooooooooooooooooooooooooooooooooooooooooooooooooo; for like 5 minutes. How many minutes until you switch off or think your audio book is stuck? Maybe a brief pause between each no?

Typically, I've had a crap night's sleep. The old shoulder pain is back from the injury I sustained during the skydive last October. Of course, it shows itself when we have to be up and on a flight, making it a longer day than normal. Oh well, what can you do but pop a couple of Ibuprofen with your breakfast muffin and crack on with the day. We don't have to be at the airport until the afternoon so we might as well see what other delights New Zealand can offer up – and it still can.

We seek out our favourite place for our morning coffee in Lyttelton which is a combo of Camden and Hampstead judging by the people who wander around. I could be wrong, but it looks like people dress like they have nothing, but on closer inspection most of the holey, scruffy clothes and boots are actually what would be classed as 'vintage'. No working class person would dress like this for fear of looking like a down and out, but in other classes it's a statement of something... opting out? Opting out, with the security of the parents' monthly payment. I know this sounds very bitchy, when actually it comes from a place of jealousy; these people look like they have the freedom to be creative and choose their path, but actually there is probably a lot of pressure on them to do well and I don't have that. Probably got that totally wrong, I know from reading about the area that they suffered badly in the earthquake and it's easy to make a judgement with only a glance and let's not forget I'm very grumpy because I'm leaving. So, I apologise if I've offended anyone.

After our lovely coffee, just like all of them in NZ, the only bad one we had was in a place across from the train station in Dunedin which professed to have won awards – they certainly wouldn't have won it for our cappuccino. No froth! Honestly. I might get a tattoo with a picture of a cappuccino with the correct ratios of coffee/milk and froth. Then I can roll up my sleeve and point to it when they deliver something that is clearly not what I asked for. Anything less and it's a latte and not a cappuccino. Oh dear, I am very grumpy today... sorry. But this is a real guide.

After I've done a double back flip off my soapbox and landed in a heap on the floor... the next port of call is Sumner, which is a suburb of Christchurch. We have driven past this every day when we've explored the Banks Peninsula. This area is beautiful, but there is a lot of construction work going on, which looks like it means business on the tourist front. Lovely cafes and shops are dotted up and down the typically grid formatted roads. The beach is to die for; everyone is enjoying it today and it's still quiet. Surfers, beach wanderers, friends, families and school kids. The beach is so big you can easily find your own little oasis and a space to reflect.

As with anyone enjoying a fantastic holiday, we wish we had more time to explore this area. I would liken it to Cornwall for the stunning beaches and surf. Not that I surf – I would attract a crowd wondering why the whales had turned up out of season!

We enjoy our last pack up and cruise in the car before washing and hoovering our trusted steed before we return it to the car hire company. It's been great, which really makes a difference to any holiday. It's sad to be handing it over after such a long time. Vehicles seem to have their own personalities and ours has certainly put up with some mileage. We started on 118,692 kilometres and ended at 124,414; so, 5,722 kilometres or 3,555 miles which is an average of 137 miles per day. Every mile has been a joy – well maybe other than the visit to the doctors and even that was dealt with quickly. After saying goodbye with a lump in my throat, we head to the airport.

Once checked-in we find a spot in the airport to relax while we wait for our flight to Sydney. Chris has checked the screens, as an announcement came over about a delay to a Sydney flight of 3 hours... please don't let it be ours. Please don't let it be ours. We have done so well so far. Sorry to wish ill on others... but when travelling this late in the day, who needs a delay as well?

Phew, it's not ours. Well, not so far. I feel bad for those affected, but pleased ours is on time. We will arrive in Sydney at 8.30pm and then have to get to our digs for the week so we definitely don't need any delays. I've experienced arriving late into places before and no shops, nothing being open and it's not a pleasant way to start a holiday. Although that's tended to be resorts in Spain or Greece and not a main city. It's an odd feeling arriving at night. There seems a sinister edge to everything; or maybe that's the tiredness. I'm sure Sydney never sleeps, just like London. I've been on Oxford Street in London at 7pm on Christmas day and shops have been open; a bit surreal on Christmas day, I have to say.

I'm currently sitting in the airport with only half an hour until boarding, reflecting on our time in New Zealand. I really don't want it to end. We've had such an amazing experience and are very lucky in lots of ways. So many things happened while we were here and just after we left which could/did affect our time here; the main one was, of course, the Christchurch massacre. *(A few weeks after we left the main bridge was washed out at Franz Josef; which would have really messed up our plans).* We had no problem with the car or the accommodation. We didn't kill each other; which is always a bit of a bonus. I really hope that one day we get to come back to this amazing country, although I'm not sure even the iCloud has enough space for any more of my photos!

Thanks for being you, New Zealand. You've been immense.

> **TOP TIP:** *Christchurch airport.... Once you've checked your bags in, if you want a bit more choice on the food front then don't go straight through security. There are not as many options; although the café is nice and does amazing sweet potato fries! Fries aside though, we thought there would be more past security but the choice for food is limited. As a bonus we got a meal on the flight from Christchurch to Sydney, with it only being a 3 and half hour flight we didn't think we'd get one. As with all the international flights they have a great selection of films to watch and the seats are comfortable and there is free alcohol.*
>
> **TOP TIP:** *Clean your boots/shoes before you leave. You will receive a form on all international flights. On the form it asks about wilderness /trekking. There are hefty fines if you mislead or lie so be truthful even if you think you will get delayed. We ticked yes to being in the wilderness – we had been on a road trip and had a rucksack full of walking boots so couldn't claim to have been sunning ourselves on a pristine yacht for the whole time. Anyway, we were sensible, and I cleaned off our boots before we left. While we were in the line, a woman came down and checked the forms before we got to security and we confirmed we'd cleaned them and that was it; she marked it okay and off we went. Better to have a delay. You wouldn't want to be responsible for bringing in something you shouldn't or the fine.*

Total Spent: *$160.44/£83*

Part Four: A City Tour

Time for the Sydney adventure to begin...

Sydney
Day 33 | Friday 22nd March

We arrive with no problems after our first flight with Emirates. I would fly with these again. Every airport has a slightly different process which no-one explains to you, but make sure you have a pen, your passport and address of the place you are staying to fill in the paperwork before you get off the plane then you will be ahead of the game.

When you arrive, if you've ticked the box to say you've been into the wilderness you have to go into a separate queue. But, be truthful – better to have a slight delay than pay a fine.

Boot check done. Sadly, we have none of the drama like in Heathrow airport with queuing. Bags collected, we catch a cab to save faffing with metros/buses. It's well worth the $30 dollars which is about £16 for the ease, and it saves crucifying our poor bodies carrying heavy rucksacks. There is also something weird about arriving into a new country at night. It's very difficult to get our bearings. A cab is a great way of clocking where shops are as you stare out of the window taking it all in.

In the cab I reach into my bag to get my purse and an insect has appeared on my fingers. I, of course, shake the little fecker off, hoping to God it hasn't bitten me and I will have to visit another doctor; this time in Australia. I will change the title to 'a guide to the best medical care around the world!' I flick the insect off and try to pretend it isn't there, moving my legs quicker than when I had to dance at a Scottish ceilidh in Jersey! I'm convinced there is a nest of insects crawling up my legs. Later in the apartment we also find a cockroach. I know Australia has its creepy crawlies, but they don't all have to all say hello on the first night! That added to the fact that a woman points out the noise of bats in the trees on the way back from the supermarket, we now need a koala to wave out of the tree and a kangaroo to hop down the street and we have nearly a full set.

Once we've dropped our bags in our apartment using a keycode to get in, which is much better than having a key to worry about losing, we shuffle outside to get supplies and immediately turn left instead of right trying to find the supermarket. I think we are drawn by the noise of people having a good time in the pubs. This place certainly looks vibrant; again, a bit like Camden but without people dressing like they are hippies from the 60's. It's a cool area – not sure I can say cool at my age, but I will.

We eventually find the supermarket; it's called Woolworths, for all you UK readers of a certain age who have a special place in our hearts for Woolworths – where you could pretty much buy anything. I'm still sad it's gone. Anyway, we discover that you cannot buy alcohol in supermarkets here, so we find a bar – if it says bottle shop on the side you can go in and buy bottles of wine, boxes of beer, and they are good prices. I get a nice bottle of fizz for about £7, so supermarket prices. We have booze to celebrate our first night, and breakfast items purchased, so return to the comfort of our air-conditioned apartment. Bliss, pure bliss, so make sure you get a place with air con if you're here when it's hot – it makes such a difference.

Content that we've made it to Australia with no problems. The insect doesn't appear to have bitten me. It was all smooth running through the airport, and in our modern apartment we recline in our comfortable bed ready to start our Australian adventure tomorrow. We are slightly sad that our New Zealand road trip has ended, but with no time to think about it now. We have Sydney to do!

Accommodation: Buxton House, Redfern, Sydney

Nights: 7

Number: 3

Type: Studio Apartment

Facilities: We have a cooker people! Fantastic apartment and facilities. Access to washing machine for free, and a clothes dryer so you can hang your washing in the garden.

Price: £512.89

Wi-fi: Free and fast

Check-In: Easy – pin number to access building and apartment

Parking: No car! Feels weird

Weather: Phew it's hot! Coming out of the airport it's like Singapore all over again

Skin colour: Still tanned

Bites: Still there, but mainly bruising. Did swell up on the plane but no medical assistance required

Bats: Why did no-one mention the giant bloody bats here! Why?

Total Spent: *$85.53/£46*

Darling Harbour and hop on/hop off
Day 34 | Saturday 23rd March

After breakfast and putting on a wash. We cross the main road to a café called, Baffi & Mo, which does beautiful coffees. Lovely feel to the place and great service. Pretty much in heaven right now. For caffeine addicted travellers this doesn't get any better. We watch the world go by and plan our first day in Sydney before going back to the apartment to start the adventure.

Washing hung out to dry on the rack provided, we make our way from Redfern and into Sydney. As I've said before these facilities are important when on the road a long time. If we hadn't chosen places with them, it would be a trip to a launderette rather than putting a wash on and luxuriating in a café, whilst waiting to hang the clothes out to dry. It does provide you with a few extra precious hours.

Turning right out of our accommodation, and then left, the road takes you with a few more little turns to Central Station. From here you follow the signs which disappear quickly, and we end up where we didn't intend, in the Darling Harbour area – which is amazing. Getting slightly lost on a trip is what it's all about – or so Chris tells me! Loads to see and do in this area. It has a variety of museums en route to the harbour and I treat myself to a new bag from one of the shops as mine has fallen apart. Jack Bauer would be proud of my bag, and I know I'm about to play a game my aunty is the master of – the zip game; zip race. I will explain…

Once on a holiday in Jersey, after I'd had a particularly heavy night out drinking anything alcoholic with my friends who live in Jersey, I had what we will call, a sensitive head. I awoke to my mum being quiet as a mouse and trying to get my aunty out of the room. My aunty had decided to get up at some ungodly hour and have a 'bloody zip race' with her suitcase – open, close, open, close, pause, open, close: I firmly told her off after my patience had run out. I don't normally get grumpy but, hey, we all have our boiling point.

Anyway, I digress…

With my contents transferred to the new bag, we partake of some very tasty sandwiches in the centre at the harbourside, and take on board some well needed water – it's approximately 24–28 degrees, but feels like 42 in the full sun and only slightly manageable in the shade with a breeze. We purchase a hop on/hop off bus deal which is our standard way of dealing with the unnatural heat in any country. How people lie in the sun all day I will never know; it must be like having a superpower. My pale white skin newly tanned skin screams louder than a vampire facing the sun..

I love hop on/hop off buses in cities. If you buy your tickets online you normally get a better deal. On the bus you show the driver your emailed purchase, and they print you out a ticket. They are a great way to get to know your locality. I've spoken before about how strange I find it to land in a new place with no idea of my location in it. Questions I ask myself is: what if a zombie apocalypse happens? How will I know where is the safest place? Where is the nearest café that does decent coffee? Where can I get food? Any food? Important facts like these need to be established early on for me to know my place in the world. Does anyone else needs this mental map of the places they visit?

First impressions of Sydney are what a cool place it is. It definitely has that vibe about it, where you can happily wander around taking in the sights and sounds all day long. Maybe chilling in a park, *(Looking out for biting insects; particularly the massive ants that could gnaw your leg off – okay slight exaggeration.)* watching the world go by and the people in it.

Taking advantage of the bus trip we do a few loops around the city to get our bearings. All the iconic sights come into view: the stunningly massive Sydney Harbour Bridge, the Sydney Opera House, an area called the Rocks which is an interesting place to visit, past the Museum of Sydney, *(Which we never get time to visit on this trip.)* the State Library of New South Wales which is an equally impressive building. *(Again another place we don't get chance to visit – I think this is all looking like we need to make a return visit.)* We only have a week here and like everywhere, it's not long enough.

Spending a good few hours enjoying the sights of Sydney, we trudge back to the apartment passing the lovely tree lined streets which offer some welcome shade. After showering and eating some food we return to Darling Harbour as they have free firework show on a Saturday night. To be honest we are both a bit tired. After a long flight yesterday, the heat and a full day sight-seeing, it's very tempting to lie down on the comfy bed and snooze. But we won't get the chance to watch the fireworks again, so off we trot, feet already complaining about the abuse they're suffering.

We spend a very pleasant few hours in a bar in the harbour. The weather is quite muggy, despite a bit of rain falling as the evening moves on. The fireworks are magical against the backdrop of the towering buildings and the lights glint off the water. It really sets the scene to our first day in Sydney. Content, we return to the apartment, which is about a forty-five-minute walk. This is the fourth time today, and my feet are right royally protesting. I know I'm going to pay for this lack of care.

What a great full day. We go to sleep looking forward to what the rest of the week has to offer.

Total Spent: *$405.94/£219*

Bus Trip day with the Hop on/Hop off

Day 35 | Sunday 24th March

Early doors we walk from our accommodation in Redfern to the collection point for the hop on/hop off bus which is near Central Station. Most of the main stops have guides where you can buy tickets and get information.

We travel through Surry Hills, Oxford Street in Woollahra before arriving at Bondi beach. We'd decided to see what all the fuss is about. To be honest it isn't for me. It's a lovely beach, and stunning location, surrounded by equally lovely and expensive houses. Maybe the fact I'm not into surfing or posing due to not having the body for it – it's not my thing. I love a scenic beach, but this one is crammed with people and that isn't our sort of beach. We stay to have a coffee, before grabbing the next hop on/hop off bus.

> **TOP TIP:** *The bus company have an app which you can download; this is useful for seeing where the bus stops are located and the rough times. They have two routes – red is the city one and blue is the one for Bondi beach.*

I don't know if I did Bondi Beach justice really, it wasn't for me at all. But, I think the heat might have played a part. I don't know the exact temperature, but it must have been close to thirty-five degrees, which is the point my body actually melts, and my brain ceases to work.

After doing a full loop around the outskirts of Bondi beach – there are some very impressive properties. I suspect you have to be more than a millionaire to live in this area. We get off at central station and patronise a café across the road called Side Bar, opting for halloumi sandwiches and, as with all the food so far, we are not disappointed, and we are grateful for the breeze that has picked up, even if it does keep knocking over our table number. It's very welcome!

Full up, we negotiate the busy road to the bus stop, and are told there is a bit of a wait due to some protests or something going off – seems the whole world is protesting nowadays.

Rant alert…

Brexit is still on everyone's lips back at home, yet the funny thing is, we have talked to loads of people on our trip and only the taxi driver in Singapore ever mentioned it. They are naturally more concerned with what's happening in their own country and with so many other things happening in the world it's not surprising. I was hoping Brexit would be all done and dusted for when we arrive back on the 1st April 2019, but it looks like the buggers are delaying it. It seems a democratic vote is not good enough when it doesn't go the way they want it. Might as well play rock, paper scissors until you get the result you want – best out of 50 anyone… Anyway, enough of that. The rich will decide and us working class will crack on, moaning about it. It won't all be decided until the rich and powerful get what they want. Borders are stupid made up human things anyway – it's one earth, people! ONE EARTH!

Phew, don't know where that rant came from – must be the heat! It's now December 2019 and I'm doing another edit of this journal and Brexit still isn't done and my country has managed yet another pointless vote; which again no-one is happy with. Promise, rant over. Now February 2020 and we are 'officially' out of the EU, well they have the whole 'divorce agreement' to sort out with the EU. What's changed so far – nothing.

Back to the bus trip…

Next stop we get off and head for the boat trip that's included in the deal. If you take the trip, you need to find the kiosk to exchange the bus ticket for a boat ticket; I will say that the general information is a bit lacking for this tour bus.

Anyway, we ask, and are rewarded and we catch our Captain Cook one-hour tour around the harbour.

Luckily for us – I seem to have said this/or thought this a lot on our trip. There are hardly any people on the boat. Timing is everything though and we arrive at Sydney Cove at around 2pm, and, as we thought, people are still at lunch. I don't know if this is the reason why it's so quiet, but we have the front of the boat to ourselves. We feel like we are on a private boat having a tour around the harbour.

The boat trip is fabulous and well worth the money. They have live commentary as we cruise around the area. They stop at a few places so you can get on/off for the Zoo, Shark Island to picnic, and Watson's Bay. The iconic views of Sydney; the Bridge, Opera House, and city skyline are a delight to see. Circular Cove, Sydney Cove, Port Jackson, and all the little beach coves look amazing – much more our kind of beaches. Sydney truly sits on a wonderful place in the world. I can see why they have the outdoor lifestyle here – how could you not with the nice weather, and this kind of world on your doorstep. The cloud comes over during the trip offering welcome relief from the sun. The temperatures have been approximately 26–29 degrees today but feel like it's 35.

Boat trip done we catch the hop on/off bus and do what you do on a bus; people watch. The people who looked knackered, like me at the end of a long day are shaking their aching feet. The ones who look a bit grumpy, just like me. I get irritated by people when I'm tired, and I don't like being touched. Chris at one point accidently brushes my arm; my glare is lost as he looks the other way.

I don't know if anyone else gets this, but when I'm hot, sweaty and tired I cannot stand people near me. If anyone else is people watching and they were to glance at the bus, they would wonder what the hell was up with me. Head resting on my arm, I look the epitome of a broken tourist.

On the inside, I'm happy as Larry.

After a full day, I gratefully recline on the bed watching a film, until it's time to switch the light off on another fabulous day. My body aches; I think I have some form of sunburn; my feet feel like they don't belong to me. It's been bloody brilliant.

Total Spent: $82.59/£45

Hop on/Hop off
Day 36 | Monday 25th March

Today I feel tired, which isn't that surprising. The achy legs of a city break are taking their toll. For the first time, I have pangs for home – in a nice, happy and contented kind of way, but I'm getting to the point where I'm ready. This place is very comfortable, but it's not home. If I could snap my fingers and arrive home to re-energise for a week, I would be back out for more. We managed to fit in some good chill days in New Zealand, but that's harder to do when you're only on the other side of the world for a week. I want to make sure I make the most of every single day.

I drag my tired Yorkshire legs to Central Station and the bus stop. The guide recognises us from yesterday and tells us it will be about twenty minutes until the next bus. We nip across the road to McDonalds for a comfort break; there seems to be a surprising lack of toilets in Sydney so far. Maybe they are all in the station? You have to ask for the key to use the facilities in quite a few of the places. Same in the café we ate in yesterday; we had to go into the hotel which I presume is all part of the same company and ask for the key from reception. Even though we are not buying anything we feel justified in using them – we are good customers of McDonalds for coffee and hangover foods. The toilets have that weird blue light which I believe are to stop junkies shooting up. It's the first time I've seen them on the trip and highlights the fact that we're back in a city. I have pangs for the roads in New Zealand, the open countryside, breathtaking mountains, crystal clear waters and quiet. *(I just sighed... I want to go back.)*

We wait at the bus stop after our interesting visit to McDonalds and listen to confused tourists – it's entertaining and passes a few minutes before we get on the first bus of the day.

> **TOP TIP**: *The bus this morning is very frustrating. If you get one of the first buses out, be prepared for the bus driver to be selling the tour tickets to people and advising them; this equals hanging about on the bus for a long time. Not every stop has one of the guides on the roadside selling and giving information. I understand that people need the information, but if you don't want to be sitting for ages then I suggest you get the slightly later bus. Normally, we wouldn't care, but having spent all day Saturday and Sunday doing the stops you've quickly listened to all the commentary; if I hear about the another biggest, tallest, longest... I will go mad.*

Once a friend and I went on the tour bus in London, I swear I think we were on it for about 10 years. We certainly felt a decade older when we left. Every time we decided to get off it changed the route and then we had to stay on to wait for our stop. We were delirious by the end and had to console ourselves with pasta and wine; lots of wine. Never ever, will we confuse London Bridge and Tower Bridge!

I digress...

Finally, we make it to our stop. I chat to an annoyed Scottish woman who says she's sick of being on the bus and wants to go to the Opera House stop and thinks they told her the wrong stop. As we got our ticket at 12.13pm and it's a 48-hour pass, we have approximately ten minutes to get to the Skytower before our ticket runs out. I feel like Anneka Rice from Treasure Hunt racing to get to the next location– fantastic programme. This attraction is included in the bus ticket price offer, as was the boat trip. It's only about a 5-minute walk from the bus stop though. You will see the sign for the Westfield centre – strange seeing a Westfield shopping centre, as they are all over the UK now. The escalators are right in front as you enter the building, and we select the fourth floor and exchange our bus ticket for the ticket to the tower. We make it just in time. Anneka would be proud.

There is a 4D short film shown first, which is actually very good, apart from a massive group of males who arrive to push in, but this woman will not be moved – thank you very much! I can push with the best of them when it's required.

We have to go through a security section before going up the tower. I guess they have this in case someone decides to blow up it up. But, it makes a bit of a mockery when the bleeper keeps going off for a bloke, and after leaving his keys and belt, it still goes off. The woman asks him if he has anything else and he says no and she lets him go in! Come on, like if he intended harm, he would confess he had a bomb, knife or gun because she'd asked! Stupid.

A fast ride up the lift makes your ears pop, and we are greeted by the fabulous sights of Sydney. This attraction is worth paying for but go with the deal with the bus and the boat as it's a lot cheaper. The city skyline are breath-taking. Chris suffers with a bit of vertigo and looking down at the ants AKA people, he has a little wave.

Next, we find the Rocks area as there are steps that lead to the Harbour Bridge from here. Initially we are not that impressed with the area as there is a lot of building work going on and it's all a little bit confusing. Finally, we find our way to the steps and walk over the Harbour Bridge; a must do whilst in Sydney. We did think about doing the guided walk over the top, but we don't have the budget for it and I'm not sure how Chris would fare with the height. It's a pleasant walk over, stopping to take pictures and remind ourselves we are on the iconic bridge; yes, we really are!

On the other side we have a bit of dilemma and are not sure what to do. We attempt to go into a restaurant for a drink, but they have finished serving. After sitting by the water underneath the Harbour Bridge, we decide to cut our losses and go back to the apartment. Our tired feet sigh gratefully at our decision, especially when we decide to get a cab because we simply cannot face walking anymore.

It's nice to have a bit of chill time in the apartment, and after dinner we check out one of the pubs in the Redfern area. All the amenities are on hand here and everyone is very friendly. There are also some great looking restaurants. We spend a little bit of time in the pub garden watching the Giant Bloody Vampire Sucking Bats that go over before dusk – I kid you not! Why did no-one tell us about the massive bats? Why is there not a public service announcement on the plane as you land? Beware new visitors, at some point Dracula and his stag do will fly over; it's nothing to be alarmed about…

Total Spent: *$141.90/£77*

Blue Mountains
Day 37 | Tuesday 26th March

Amazing trip to the Blue Mountains today, well worth a visit if you get the opportunity. Getting the train tickets is slightly confusing, as there is no information in Central Station and no-one to ask. We wanted to buy an Opal card as this seems the cheapest option, but we couldn't see anywhere to get one so ended up using the machine to buy two single tickets – the machine is easy to use though. If we'd thought about it, we should have dropped into the station and collected an Opal card when we had more time or from one of the information desks dotted around the city. You can buy the Opal cards from newspaper vendors, but we didn't know this at the time. Anyway, it was still only $20.80 each for a return or £11 each and the train is a two hour train journey, unless you the get the express one that doesn't stop at every stop.

The trains are cool as they are the double decker style ones. We've been on these in Amsterdam before and we don't have these in the UK, due to our Victorian bridge building past, we don't have the room for them. Instead we have single carriages trundling across a crap track and pay a fortune for the privilege! Sorry, moaning about the UK again. Also, the seats rotate so you can change your direction of travel, which is pretty darn cool.

The journey is long at two hours and it gives our bodies a well-needed bit of rest. It's interesting to look at the suburbs of Sydney, how people live as we all do in the modern world. It's not so different on the other side of the world. That's the surprising element to this trip, how everything really isn't so different. I suppose we have only visited westernised places and other than some feeling like it's in a by-gone era and, in the case of New Zealand, all the scenery being more epic, general day to day life is the same wherever you go in the world; if you're lucky enough to live in the modernised world; or unlucky enough some people think.

Some girl decides to have a breakfast which consists of a very smelly egg! REALLY!

During the long journey it's nice to have the time to sit and reflect on Sydney and the area we are staying in. I can highly recommend our accommodation, and the Redfern area in general. Surrounded by coffee shops, convenience shops and fantastic pubs, this is a good place to base yourself. It's only about a 15–20 minute walk to Central Station and about 5–7-minute walk to Redfern Station. Redfern feels like a place that has been in a rough relationship and is emerging into something better, a stronger and cleaner version of its old self, without losing the essence of the place. This feeling is generally something that cannot be made. I find the places with the best vibes have evolved, maybe without intention, into what they are.

Arriving at Katoomba station it's a bit of a scramble to get our pre-paid tickets from the booth at the top of the stairs. One of the blokes gives one couple so much information I don't think they need to go on the tour, and he does this regardless of the massive queue. Chris gets the tickets while I get the coffee *(It's been two hours!)* and finally tickets in hand, we cross the street to catch the bus.

We buy hop on/hop off tickets with all the extras *(I typed sextres then – it's not that kind of book!)* the activities are worth adding to your trip. So many things to do including; cable cars, scenic railway, skyway and walkways. They are exhilarating and good fun. There are lots of walks to do around the area, as with most of the places we've been you need another three weeks to explore and even then you will still not see everything.

Our driver, Jimmy is a fountain of knowledge on the area and funny to boot. Great tour guide and can speak many languages. He offers to take a rare photo of us at a photo stop. These guys really do know their stuff, so to get the best out of the day, ask them. Scenic World is great fun. The rides can be enjoyed by anyone, and our tickets allows us unlimited rides. We sadly only have chance for a couple of the stops around the Blue Mountains, and we opt for the cascades and waterfall which are beautiful. Word of warning though there are many many steps.

All of the stops are well laid out with easy to hard walking options, and long to short walks. The views will be amazing, so it doesn't matter which one you choose to do.

The views over the Blue Mountains are stunning. If you to find a quiet moment, take a seat away from everyone else and lose yourself in the vista, listen to the constant bird song and just 'be' for a minute.

After another fabulous day, we make our way for a drink and some food and then return to the station. Sitting outside enjoying something to eat, means, the inevitable wasp turns up to annoy everyone that has dared to try and sit outside. I know I keep saying this, but you could easily do a week in this area alone; there is so much to see. If you can squeeze a couple of days then go for it, better still if you can stay around the area rather than have your base in Sydney. It will give you an extra four hours where you're not travelling.

On the train home, I reflect that we only have a few days left to go now until this epic journey is at an end. I'm looking forward to looking through all my pictures and this journal when editing and adding to it and reliving all that has happened.

It's now February 2020 and I'm getting towards the final editing of this journal, ready to unleash it onto the world! I cannot wait to have our adventures in print, but it's also making me sad as I cannot wait to return.

Total Spent: *$294.35/£159*

Manly and massive spiders!
Day 38 | Wednesday 27th March

The morning is spent chilling and updating this journal, after a long day yesterday we plan to visit Manly this afternoon.

We break the chilling to sneak in a visit to Baffi & Mo's and grab a coffee which we take to the park about thirty seconds from our apartment. The noise of the various birds doesn't make for a peaceful park walk if that's what you're after, but it is interesting. The Bin Ends *(Australian White Ibis.)* parrots, magpies, and good old pigeons, a staple for any park, are going about their day. If you're into birds and trees, then look no further than this park if you're staying in the Redfern area. The grass is being mowed as we sit enjoying our coffees and it smells like an English summer, making me long for home, whilst not wanting to leave.

I see on the news that New Zealand is getting its unfair share of trouble in the form of storms. Less than two weeks ago we were in the area where the bridge has been washed away. Once again, we feel grateful for our holiday timings; we have been very lucky throughout our trip. I feel sorry for the people trapped by the storms. How long it will take to repair the bridge is anyone's guess. I cannot believe the trickle of water we saw in some rivers has taken out a main bridge. The power of nature! Mess with her at your peril. We are having to deal with the power of mother nature now with the new virus that has hit the world!

Chilling and coffees done, we return to Redfern station to get the train to Circular Quay. Again, we should have got one of those Opal cards, but you can buy a single easy enough and it's only about £2.30 each way. I would advise you to check out what you are doing before you catch the train – there never seems to be anyone around to ask or help, and even though they have the screens for the trains and they are clear and easy to use and the stations are straight forward, as a tourist you're always a bit more mindful of getting it wrong and sometimes just need someone to confirm that you're going in the right direction, with the right ticket.

It's about a 10–15 minute ride to Circular Quay. We wish we used this sooner and saved our legs, but walking the streets is a good way of getting to know an area and the walk to Central Station is pretty much a straight road from our accommodation if you don't get lost. There is also the chance you might spot Dracula and his mates as you're meandering along, depending on the time of day.

At Quay 4 we buy our tickets for the fast ferry to Manly. Lucky for us there is a ferry already in. They are every twenty minutes, so not long to wait if you miss one. The ferry is pleasant, and again we take in the sights of iconic buildings and structures that seem part of our daily life now, and dare I say it, it almost seems to take the mystery away from them. I've heard about Sydney from friends who have visited and obviously seen the New Year's Eve Celebrations and the iconic symbols, then suddenly you've arrived, and you've seen them for yourself. I wonder at the power of the internet, tv and phones that maybe take some of the magic out of it because you've already seen it and know what to expect. When you first see these iconic places, it is amazing and wonderful, but, I don't know about anyone else, I soon get used to them.

Obviously, the experience is different, and you get to say 'you've been there', a bit like Hobbiton for me. Once you've seen it/done it then naturally you move onto the next item on the list that you want to see or do. It's a human's curiosity that makes us do so much and strive to see things.

Chris and I feel incredibly lucky to have all the experiences we've had so far in our lives, and we have explored a fraction of the places some of our friends have visited.

Appreciating the good times in life is very important to us. I would rather acknowledge it now, than look back in years to come and wish I had. Anyway, enough of that, it's not a self-help book!

Arriving in Manly we find the beach. It's a cloudy overcast day which we are grateful for; the temperature is perfect. We snap a couple of pictures and satisfy our caffeine addiction. We sit on a bench overlooking Manly beach and take in the sights. Already I prefer Manly to Bondi. Maybe because today it's a bit quieter and cooler. Some places just have that air about them which is difficult to recreate artificially – as I've already mentioned.

We make for the North Head Point for a coastal walk.

> **PUBLIC SERVICE ANNOUNCEMENT:** *If you're in any way scared of spiders, do not, I repeat DO NOT do this walk. You start with a gentle walk around the bay, to the left and up some steps. At the top you might be able to glimpse some of the birds that hang around up here. You're treated to lovely views of the coastline, some great photo opportunities. At the top you're also greeted by webs and spiders which have red stripes – as in danger – you will die. I still don't understand why there is not a huge neon sign saying 'Massive bloody spiders' – similar to one that should have one for bats. Anyway, as Chris points out we are in Australia and they are known for the creepy crawlies.*

To start the journey now you've been warned…

Taking a few pictures, we decide to do the circular headland walk back into Manly. There are clear steps cut into the hillside and although it gets the old heart rate pumping, it's a pleasant walk through the trees, until you get to Shelob's lair – if you don't know who Shelob is, where have you been and why haven't you read Lord Of The Rings? Anyway, she is a massive spider. Another couple on the walk decide they are huntsman spiders, which is very worrying as I'm sure they are very bad spiders! *(Later we find out they are orb spiders, yeah, not poisonous but scary as hell.)* The web span across the trees is immense, my mum comments on my photo later and she's correct in her interpretation of the picture – it does look like a curtain of web with the massive bloody spiders in the middle waiting to eat any unsuspecting tourist that foolishly enters their domain.

We carefully explore the rest of this route. There are plenty of spiders along the way, but we give each other respect and space and don't bother each other. The whole right side of the walkway seems to have been burnt out. *(I find out later that this is part of the Manly Scenic walkway. The burning is controlled, to avoid random burning during the hot season, and control the landscape.)* I think it's a way to get rid of the spiders, but it creates the most eerie landscape. Swampy wet areas in some parts are in stark contrast to the dry arid areas, which make you feel like you're on another planet.

Coming to the end, thankful we are still alive, we walk downhill back into Manly. School children are making their way home and are probably used to the sight of sweaty tourists looking grateful that they've survived the 'spider walk'. It is worth doing – even the scary spiders provide us with an experience we wouldn't get at home. Again it makes us realise we are on the other side of the world, it's easy to forget we are so far away.

The blue skies have returned, and we find the beach front once again and sit in a bar to watch the world go by. They have a few happy hour offers here from about 3–4pm and 6–7pm. Word to the wise; the rose wine is a bit strong! After drinks we use our sat nav noses to find a place Chris found on the internet. It promises amazing fish and chips and tempura vegetables. It does not disappoint. *(I will regret this decision later at night when my stomach has swollen to the size of one of the spider's abdomens if they were the size of*

Shelob. Thankfully we bought a lot of indigestion tablets – the food was delicious and well worth the discomfort.)

Satisfied physically and well fed, we catch the train to Redfern, and it's full of workers doing their commute home. They probably don't care that they are in Sydney, it's their normal place of work or place to live. I wonder how many times they look up and appreciate where they are.

Wearily we walk back from the station but first we stop for a drink in what is now our local – the Tudor pub – highly recommended. They are really friendly, the downstairs outside bit is a bit smoky for us, but we go up the metal steps to the right and there is a nice rooftop area. This is the place we came to our first night in Sydney in need of a pack of beer and a bottle of wine. We've only been in Australia five full days, but it feels longer.

We reflect on another great day before heading to the apartment for tea and to put our feet up.

Total Spent: *$188.37/£102*

Last day in Sydney
Day 39 | Thursday 28th March

I'm writing this on Thursday morning, our last day in Sydney, as we have to leave early tomorrow morning for our flight. The sun is shining and I'm typing away in the garden area of our apartment while Chris plays on his game. I can hear people shouting, 'IT'S YOUR LAST DAY' Get out and DO something!' We will later, but we have boring things like some washing to do/pre-pack. I also admit to having the end of holiday tiredness. I know you're shouting, 'For God's sake man up!' But, I can hear my sofa calling me home. Six weeks away has been enough.

Friends of mine have gone away for 6 months to over a year. It's not for me. Don't try and do something because someone else has. As much as we've loved our time away, much more than I thought, I'm ready for my home comforts. I could quite easily do a week at home and then another six weeks away mind.

Just a quick update on the bites before we start the day...

Sand fly bites reduced to skin scars. Bites: 6 news ones – bitten by who knows what! Three on my ankle where they could find space the sand flies had left. Two on my arm and one on my leg. *(By bedtime the one on my arm and leg is about the size of coaster. Chris shakes his head, incredulous that I keep constantly getting things wrong with me. He's not alone, that's the only thing that has been bad about this trip and, even then, it's not stopped me doing anything.)*

It's our usual morning in Redfern, wake up, have a drink in bed before I make a breakfast of scrambled egg on wholemeal muffin. Showers done, we go across the road for a coffee, which we take to the park and amuse ourselves watching the wildlife. The rest is spent doing washing and the pre-pack. We both have that last day feeling, where you feel like you should be rushing around, but also feeling the effects of a trip coming to the end. We want to tackle the Botanical Gardens later for the dusk migration of the bats we've become obsessed with.

Finally, we decide to brave the heat of the day and head out for our last hours in Sydney. It's about 26–27 degrees in the full sun today. I can feel it sapping my energy as we make our way on the familiar route to Redfern station.

We try to buy a ticket from the self-serve machine in the station and after three attempts and having to move so others could use it due to them only having one machine and no-one to ask, we buy a ticket to the station on the route and get on the train. Our destination is Rose Bay. We had thought about going back to Manly as we liked it so much, but thought it was best to try somewhere new.

Arriving at the station we go to buy another ticket and cannot find Rose Bay on the options. After finding an actual human being to ask. *(Hurrah.)* She's lovely – I do wish there were more staff to ask. Even though it's all in English, and although it's our first international holiday we have travelled a lot, it's still a little confusing. I'm surprised they don't have more staff to ask with it being a major tourist destination.

She tells us that it's a bus we have to get and not a train which is why we cannot find the destination on the machine. I'm sure she said you have to have an Opal card for any bus trip. We go to the newsagents she points to in the station and purchase one. Not all newsagents sell them. You pay an initial deposit of $10 to get the card and it's topped up with that amount. The minimum you can top up is $10. Rookie mistake as we really should have got one on our first day. They are the same as the Oyster card in London and you can use them on the ferries as well; so train, bus and ferry. It deducts as you use it and you top them up at the machine. The only thing is whatever you don't use, you lose, so make sure you try to have a zero or minimal balance when you leave. Anyway, it still works out okay financially to get one even if it's our last day.

The station signs direct us upstairs to the bus area and we catch a very full bus to Rose Bay. We wander along the beach and find a café to sit and have a drink and get out of the baking sun to come up with a plan. Chris has been a bit on the grumpy side and I have too. I haven't retaliated as I normally would as I know it's last day blues. Having found Rose Bay, we decide it's not for us; more for locals I would say. Cutting our losses, we catch the ferry and have a lovely journey back to Central Quay coming up with a plan for the rest of the day.

> **TOP TIP**: *If you're not bothered about commentary on the tourist boats, then get an Opal card and use the normal ferries to get around. I think one journey cost us about $3 which is approximately £1.50, and you still get the amazing views of Sydney Opera House and Bridge but fewer tourists and you can just enjoy the views.*

Arriving into Central Quay we make our way to the Botanical Gardens. Again if you don't mind massive spiders then this is a beautiful place to visit – and free! Well worth a wander around and again you're never far from the views of the Opera House and Sydney Bridge with the tall office buildings in the background. Partway around there is a little mobile café and we stop for an alcoholic beverage and toast our holiday and last day, with the sun twinkling off the water; what could be better? Because I'm so classy I put my plastic glass of prosecco in my shoe to keep it upright. *(Watch out for the giant ants when you find somewhere to sit.)*

> **TOP TIP**: *For those struggling with data you can also get free Wi-Fi in the Botanical Gardens.*

After a lovely few hours exploring the gardens, we walk to the Rocks area of Sydney which has quaint shops and cobbled streets. Like most cities there is a lot of construction work going on, so as I said earlier, we didn't immediately warm to this area when we first wandered around it. But after spending some time here, we soon understand the area. Some streets do feel like you've wandered onto a building site; but, again that's most cities.

Most of the shops are closing down for the night due to the time we've arrived. Circular Quay looked so different yesterday, and we've realised this was due to no cruise ships being docked. I've decided that they should ban them, it gives you such a different view of the harbour without a massive ship to block it; I will write a letter. We wonder if this is why the shops seem to be shutting earlier than normal.

We find a lovely Italian restaurant for our last evening meal. Chris finds a friend in one of the little starlings. Not sure it's that chuffed with the salty garlic bread as it enjoys a drink from one its secret stashes in between some stones and under leaves in the cobbled road after it's eaten it. Fed and happy, we slowly make our way to Circular Quay for our last train journey in Sydney.

It's sad walking back to our apartment, past areas that have quickly felt like home. Redfern is definitely a mix of Camden and Hampstead. The rich and wealthy rub shoulders with people who don't have a much, judging by some of the back streets. Some of the cafes are very much like the ones in Camden. They have aimed for shabby chic but managed to create shabby shit in some of them. Some are great; give me a bottle of bleach and some paint; it wouldn't take much. Overall though, the cafes are great and even the shabby shit ones do amazing coffee. The bakery and shops are handy for all your needs. It's definitely a place to visit.

Familiar and exotic, being on the doorstep of Asia, I'm surprised by how strong the communities are here. I'm not seeing a lot of what you would call the 'newer Australians', the descendants of the colonists who were sent to this so-called backwater back in the day. I thought it was down to it being a city, the cities in the UK have a more diverse cultures than most of the villages and towns here.

That's it, our final outings into Sydney done and dusted. Arriving back home *(Our apartment.)* I do a little bit more packing before closing the curtains, switching out the lights and prepare to dream about my sofa and bed.

Total Spent: *$156.36/£85*

I went and said it!
Day 40 | Friday 29th March

Using the Uber app, we order a cab. I'm impressed by the service but its $10 more than the cab into Sydney... maybe time of day? Or maybe paying for the service? We grab our last drink from the café across the road. *(Obviously.)* We will be sad to leave Sydney and the Redfern area. It's been an amazing holiday with so much more to offer.

Check-in at the airport is a nice experience and we have a good chat with the woman; she cannot believe we want to stay in Sydney and tells us that they have cold winters and have no insulation in their houses due it being warm most of the year. *(I looked it up and their cold times tend to get to about 8 degrees; we would be happy with that in the UK during winter!)*

There are big queues to the automatic passport machines, slide your passport in and wait for the barrier to open, stand and stare at a screen until another door opens to accept you into a new secure area. Then it's onto security. I've given up taking everything out unless someone notices. I think these places are more for show than anything.

Once without meaning to, I grabbed a carrier bag as I was leaving the house – I wouldn't do that nowadays now they have a value to them... Anyway, it wasn't until I got through airport security and got the bag out that I realised there was a replacement blade for a Stanley knife in there – oops. So, this had gone through screening and nothing! Although, obviously I'm glad as they probably wouldn't have let me fly. We've just flown home from Fuerteventura, and they managed to find our jar of sauce we stashed in the rucksack. We got the lecture about only having 100ml, blah blah blah. They only do it to make you buy loads of stuff in the airport.

All of the airport staff have been lovely and friendly. I don't know what it is about some of the UK airports, especially East Midlands. I think I've only encountered one nice member of staff there and the rest look as miserable as sin and are waiting to tell you off for not taking your belt off or some other pointless thing. Great impression tourists must get of the UK when they deal with our lot. *(I did meet a lovely lady going through security in East Midlands on our way back from Fuerteventura in Feb 2020. Inevitably the automatic machine didn't work so I had to deal with a real person – maybe there is hope for East Midlands yet.)*

I digress as usual...

We get through the airport shenanigans and find a place to sit and wait for our plane, and I say it, I know I shouldn't, but I do... 'We're lucky not to have had any delays.' Chris tells me off and rightly so, as, once boarded, the pilot tells us there has been a problem with the air traffic control – turns out a faulty battery started to smoke creating the evacuation of the air traffic control. I would like to say sorry officially to all the planes that were diverted and any delays – obviously my fault due to using those fatal words, erm, sorry.

The delay isn't so bad. Some people seem really annoyed, whereas I'm chilled, watching a film, with a glass of wine in my hand. People are way too quick to flip out. Look at the positives, but that could have been the wine talking. The delay doesn't last too long and we are soon on our way.

Total Spent: *$53.70/£29*

Sydney to Singapore
Day 40 | Friday 29th March

Disembarking we head into the terminal with its throng of people and bright lights, which is a little disorientating. But for those who have not travelled before it must be intimidating, in arrivals it feels like you're actually leaving the airport, but never fear… you will come to the queue for security eventually. They don't do automated check-in desks here and the sounds of multiple stamps pounding the books will be your companion until it's your turn. This is the one where you must put your thumbs on the screen to be allowed entry.

Arriving in Singapore, I thought the heat of New Zealand and Sydney would have somehow acclimatised us to the weather here. No. No, that is not the case. At the taxi rank the doors open, and the giant hot hairdryer of Satan's breath washes over us. Quickly, we realise it's no different to the day we started our amazing journey.

Suddenly it has that feel to it… that we have barely been away five minutes and not the 40 days of epicness we have experienced. I'm ready for home though. I've loved this experience and it's exceeded my expectations in many ways. I know I'm tempting fate with this, but everything has gone so well for us and whatever goes wrong now, at least we are at the end of our travels. *(I hope I don't regret this!)*

> **TOP TIP:** *For international flights you will be given a slip of paper to fill in when you arrive. You have to hand this over with your passport at security. It asks for name, DOB, where you're staying, how long for, and passport number. So, to make life easier, have a pen in your bag and keep your passport and hotel/connecting details to hand so you can fill this in on the plane – just saves a bit of time. I know I mentioned it earlier but it's well worth another mention.*

We arrive late at our hotel and after a quick check in and a basic unpacking of cases *(Opening them.)* we get some snacks from the petrol station as we are too tired to do anything else, and need to get some sleep so we are fresh for tomorrow.

Accommodation: Destination Hotel – Singapore
Nights: 2
Number: 905
Type: Superior Queen Room with breakfast
Facilities: Bedroom only. Roof swimming pool. Lovely and great views of Singapore.
Price: £186.00
Wi-fi: Free and fast
Check in: Easy
Parking: N/A
Weather: Bloody hot and bloody humid
Bites: Calmed down after I hit them with my medicinal arsenal of painkillers, alcohol, allergy tablets and indigestion tablets to soak up the effects. Although they did swell up on the plane!

Total Spent: $41.23/£23

Singapore

Day 41 | Saturday 30th March

Breakfast in the hotel is an interesting affair. Most of the guests are using chopsticks to eat everything, including one woman eating her croissant with them, I find myself fascinated as she picks up an apple with her hand wondering if she has special powers to eat it using chopsticks, but disappointingly she holds it the normal way. We ponder if it's the first time the woman has eaten; although it doesn't look like it. I would sound nasty and cruel saying she might need a trip to Weightwatchers, if I wasn't already planning on joining back up when I return to the UK. She's obviously indulged herself as I have. It looks like one of the last meals before you start your diet on Monday!

The breakfast is in turn disappointing and surprising. There is an array of food that doesn't even look like food, a bit like when you walk around the food centres here. This for me is the biggest cultural difference. A lot of it looks like leftovers from a meal and something I would chuck in the bin. I've got more adventurous as I've got older with food, but I still like to know what it is and where it has come from. Some of the other customers look happy, said lady is managing to line up her food before she's even swallowed the next one the another morsel is ready to go; it's impressive.

We manage to find some westernised breakfast items and enjoy our toast and jam with a chocolate croissant. Who doesn't like a chocolate croissant in the morning? The coffee leaves a lot to be desired with two cappuccinos looking like they are different entities altogether. One has all the milk, the other all the coffee and we give it a miss. It's our first bad coffee experience and to be honest its appropriate as I cannot wait to switch on my coffee machine at home and knock up a cappa – I wonder if it's missed us or enjoyed its break away from our constant demands.

I'm currently sitting on a chaise longue looking out on the moody skies of Singapore. Rain and thunderstorms are forecast all day. This morning we opened the curtains to lightning flashes and thunder – reminding us of our stay in Valencia last summer where it was very hot and every night they had the most amazing thunderstorms. We had a high floor in that hotel and would switch off the lights and watch nature's light show, showing us how it's really done.

My thoughts cannot help but be drawn back to home. Maybe the mind's way of dealing with it. I cannot believe that after forty days we are back in Singapore about to return home and all that will bring; crushing debts, a new job for me, and a diet. This experience has been phenomenal and if you're thinking about starting your adventure, then go for it.

I could quite happily sit here all day, writing this up with half of my mind on thoughts of home and the other on stories that have formed in my mind during the trip. I cannot wait to get back to my children's fantasy story; the experience in the Glow Worms caves has fuelled my imagination for the world I started to create. Depending when you read this it might be out – your kids might be clutching a glow worm teddy after buying one of my merchandising products when it's turned into a blockbuster… I think jetlag, ideas of grandeur or simple desperation of trying to make money rather than go to a boring job might be setting in! Also my psychological thriller is waiting patiently to be submitted to more book agents.

Right, Chris is getting restless, and making attention noises, so I better get myself into gear and get ready. If I had the body I would probably go out in a bikini – anything else is overdressed in this heat. I really don't know how people move here; I just cannot handle this kind of humidity. I would struggle with a week in Singapore, and not just because of the weather. I enjoyed the bus trip we did when we first arrived in February, but the rest is not for me.

The road trip around New Zealand will be my lasting memory. Cruising in the car, stopping for butties and ginger beer overlooking a view, and man the views! That for me is a holiday experience. A city is a long weekend to enjoy as I soon feel hemmed in by the concrete towers and throngs of people. Give me a quiet beach with lapping waves, the sun hiding behind wispy white clouds, and a gentle breeze caressing my skin, views of snow-topped mountains in the background and the promise of an amazing drive. That is bliss.

Told you something's getting to me. Right, to get ready and go and explore the city. Our last day as tomorrow we leave early for our flight back home. Back to the shores of the UK and the shit shower that is Brexit. Maybe we will never be allowed out again. "Sorry me duck the borders are shut. There's nowt' getting out, or in." Hurrah!

In a weird sort of way, I'm looking forward to what my next job will be. Each time I've changed jobs a new path has come along. I've run private day nurseries; been a nanny, *(Not like Mary Poppins – I can shuffle cards above my head but that's pretty much it for magic tricks.)* worked in a bookshop; been a mortgage underwriter; library assistant; self-employed wheeler and dealer; a self-published author – writing will be something I will always do. What will be next...

Right, properly going now – might have to seriously edit some of this ranting...

I might revise what I said about staying in Singapore. We found a little area close to the hotel – basically across the road, go left for 5 minutes and you come to the Kampong Glam area, which is beautiful. All your senses will be used when meandering these streets; the noise of the tourist;

shops selling their wares; people eating; motorbike; the smell of the many varieties of food available. If it wasn't so humid, I could wander these streets all day. This area is well worth a visit.

We decide it's too hot to attempt the Gardens by the Bay. If I really wanted to go, I would make the effort but once you've been to Barcelona and seen the Magic Fountain of Montjuic display – wow. I don't think anything can compare to how good that was.

Chris finds a Mexican restaurant he fancies and it's something we haven't eaten whilst we've been away. If you like Mexican food, then I can recommend this place. The food is delicious at Piedra Negra – I recommend the guacamole as well. They prepare it at your table and it's very tasty. We while away some time enjoying the last meal of our adventure. Before returning to our hotel for some air-conditioning and another shower.

> **TOP TIP:** *Hot off the press: be careful with taps when abroad. I think some of the plumbers have a bit of a laugh and connect the wrong ones. We've stayed in a few places now where what should be cold is actually hot water – makes for an interesting shower. I suggest you double check first. This has probably come to mind as you need to have a shower every ten minutes in Singapore.*

Total Spent: $127.90/£72

Going home
Day 42 | Sunday 31st March

We wake up to the sound of a screaming baby somewhere, standard to get woken up early on the days you have to go somewhere. But it's 6.30am so we get up and go for an early breakfast, interested to see what delights await us.

Typically, the coffee machine is being faffed with by a member of staff. Unless you are really desperate, and I always am for a coffee as you know, I wouldn't bother with the hot drinks here. The breakfast is good this morning, mainly because we're early and it's quiet. We did try all different types of options and ended up with six cups of coffee just like yesterday, none of which we drink. I hate wasting food or drink. People go mad at hotels and always seem to have bulging plates and leave half of it – rude and wasteful. But, quite frankly the drinks machine is awful, and I'm going home today and I'm grumpy, so there.

After breakfast without coffee, it's time to pack and get our last flight of this amazing trip. We have a mixture of emotions, both sad that the adventure has come to an end, and looking forward to home and the comforts it brings. As I've said I'm looking forward to my sofa, coffee machine and tv shows. Chris is desperate to see his motorbike again and has set it as his screen saver on his phone.

Probably not much more to add to today, unless something doesn't go smoothly… here's hoping for an easy, stress free end to the holiday. The taxi driver is a delight to talk to en route to the airport; we have a great chat about everything during the journey; as you do. Brexit is brought up for the first time. It's interesting to hear what people from other countries think. You also realise how it might be a big deal for us, but other countries are just cracking on as normal. He tells us a bit about Singapore, and it has a broad range of temperatures 25 – 32 degrees! It's now autumn here and only a few brown leaves tell you that the season is different. Other than those there will be little to tell you it's autumn. The driver tells us he wants to bring his family to the UK but is worried about Brexit – I tell him to crack on and ignore all the drama. The worst that could happen is you might have to get a visa – so what – we had to get a visa for some of this trip and back in the day we had to get them to travel abroad. If you listened and waited for the politicians and governments of this world, we would never get anything done! We also cover the general miss-information of the media, and the general population who are basically herded by the press. Yes, it was one of those kinds of taxi rides – very enjoyable friendly ranting on both parts.

The airport check-in goes smoothly. Changi is such a nice airport, and we have a lovely chat with the information guides they have wandering the airport. These people know how to run an airport. Why can't it be a pleasurable experience in every airport? They have a butterfly house, a free cinema, proper food quarters… I vote that they run all the airports.

***

We arrive late into the UK on what I think is still Day 42, after a bit of a bumpy flight in places but I like turbulence so I didn't mind. I try not to sleep so I can hit my hotel bed and try and catch up on the time difference. Everyone says this is the best way to deal with it and I agree.

We navigate the hustle and bustle of security and claim our baggage. It doesn't matter where you stand someone will inevitably stand in front of you. We negotiate the confusing signage to try and get the bus transfer from Heathrow. I think they are free if you can ever find the bus station. It's about £5 each to get the bus which is near the taxi rank. We decide sod it and go for the taxi – why break a habit of a holiday? It cost about £12 but worth it not to have to faff with bags and we are tired.

The check-in at the Ibis hotel is quick and we gratefully slip into our beds.

Total Spent: *$31.80/£14 UK: £12*

The End
Day 43 | Monday 1st April

(I'm typing this in Kings Cross Station on Monday 1st April – but it's not a joke that we have finally finished our trip, and Brexit still hasn't been decided.)

The breakfast in the hotel is very good including the coffee, and after indulging, we sadly leave and catch the bus which is conveniently right outside the Ibis Hotel we are staying in. It's predictably bloody freezing and I feel grumpy. Arriving at St Pancras we sit in the Wetherspoons pub. It seems odd that we are back here, where we started our travels wondering what was going to happen. What were we going to experience? Would this trip of a lifetime be everything we wanted? Lots and lots of questions that we now have the answer to. Yes, is the answer to most of them.

It feels very weird to be back in the UK after all this time. Already we're talking about our next adventure. *(After a few months at home we decide this trip might have ruined our lives as all we want to do is go again; but we are not millionaires, so you know – bit of a problem.)*

We feel incredibly lucky that we have only had a few minor problems whilst away. We've been lucky with the weather, our choices of accommodation, flights and other events that have happened during our travels which haven't affected our holiday. Some of this is down to good planning and some of it's luck. We feel grateful for the experience and I cannot wait to look at this journal, our photos and all the physical mementoes we have brought home as well as the memories.

I waffle on a little bit more in the next chapter.

Accommodation: Ibis Styles Hotel (Heathrow)
Nights: 1
Number: 405
Type: Queen Room with breakfast – Breakfast is really nice
Facilities: Kettle
Price: £55.00
Wi-fi: Doesn't work on level 4 due to it being a new hotel? Someone has also fitted a floor in the room which is as creaky as a hundred-year-old house!
Check in: Easy
Parking: N/A
Weather: Cold– can see our breath when we head for the bus in the morning. Sucks
Bites: One large one my leg – which is a new one I picked up in Singapore. Didn't want to miss out and not have a bite from every continent we visited! Good job I had my vaccinations before we came away.

Total Spent: *£20*

The End... with a P.S. and a P.P.S...

Well the holiday is over. New Zealand has been amazing, friendly, stunning, beautiful, glorious, fabulous, lovely, breath-taking… and Singapore and Sydney weren't so bad either!

Normally when I edit a book I check for repeated words and try and remove or replace, but I'm leaving in the lot, because quite frankly New Zealand deserves them all. For the geeks like me, here are the totals for how many times I've used them. Editors everywhere are weeping and snapping their red pens in half! The beauty of self-publishing.

Beautiful: 44
Amazing: 55
Breath-Taking: 11 *(11 only eleven! What!)*
Stunning: 56
Friendly: 34
Fabulous/Fab: 44
Glorious: 5
Lovely: 54
Nice: 52
Wow: 19
Coffee/cappa/cappuccino: 94 times 😊

Now I do have to add a disclaimer for any errors in this book. If you end up 187 Kilometres out of your way then don't blame me if I've given you incorrect information. I'm going to claim it's down to my medical problems so don't give me a bad review! I hope the 'TOP TIPS' make your journey that little bit easier.

It's August in 2019 and I've finally got to this point in my first edit. I feel like I have relived all of the holiday and even feel emotional about it. I really wish I could pack my bags and set off again on this amazing journey. My heart aches in a happy way at the thought of packing the bags, making the butties and setting off to explore. We have a plan to travel to visit NZ again in a couple of years but due to time and finances it won't be as long. Well unless I get an international best seller of course, or win the lotto. Long gone are the days when I could sell my body; I would have to pay them nowadays.

Anyway, I digress…

Travelling around the world is a strange experience, you realise how small the world is, but at the same time how big it is. So many millions of people going about their lives and being concerned with their circle of life.

I hope you have enjoyed our travel journal, if you want to read anything else by me, then please check me out on Amazon…

My website has a selection of pictures from the trip:

Website: clpeache.com
Instagram: c_peache
Twitter: c_peache
Chris's: NONE – he doesn't like social media!

The last pages are all about the costs… who doesn't want to know the price of an apple in New Zealand or the price of crunchie from the other side of the world?

P.S.

It's now December 2019. This is how long it takes to get started on editing and faffing, getting a cover done and then more editing. I hope you love the cover. I adore it. In February it will be a year since we set off on our travels. A whole year, but a lifetime's memories are stored.

P.P.S.

March 2020 and it's done. If you're reading this then I've finally managed to get my story out to the world. I hope you've enjoyed it and if you do travel to New Zealand say a little hello from us. If you tag my book in New Zealand I will love you forever.

Keep exploring, keep learning, keep having fun and keep the cappuccinos coming!

Happy Adventures... xxx

TOP TIPs plus

For reference...

Check your medical excess on your policy before you buy. It varies to see a doctor – it cost me $177 approximately £100. My excess is £175 so I cannot claim this back.

Print every single document and read the small print! It will make everything run a lot smoother having all the information printed; from car hire to accommodation.

Our accommodation was all pre-booked on booking.com, and all had free cancellation; most up until a few days/weeks before arrival. I would recommend doing this as soon as you have booked your flights. We changed our accommodation plans a few times after our initial booking, but some were sold out, or prices had gone up dramatically in the short space of time, so the earlier, the better. Having free cancellation gives you some flexibility to change your plans whilst away.

Make sure your mobile phone is unlocked then you can buy a SIM card from any of the Spark shops in NZ. The wi-fi in most places was pretty good, so you could get away with not having mobile data – but as I'm a phone addict I had to have it.

Accommodation...

Check it has cooking facilities even if it says it's a studio. In the UK, I would say most accommodation classed as a studio would have some kind of cooking facility. A lot only had a microwave, kettle and toaster and no hob. Also, most say no to cooking strong smelling food in them, e.g. curries, fish. It limits what you can cook if you only have a microwave and cannot cook smelly food!

One room booking said they had a washing machine. We assumed this was in the room as it was listed in the room details – it was actually for everyone to use and payable in a shared area. Difficult to check some of these things as the information can be a bit vague. Just something for you to be aware of – it's only about $10 to have one load washed and dried but that's $10 too much if you think it's with the room and free. Most of the places had access to laundry facilities which are usually coin operated. So worth saving a few $1 and $2 to save asking for change. They also sell laundry detergent for between $1-$2 dollars per wash. I bought my own tablets as I have eczema and am allergic to some powders. *(Of course I am, by now you have read about my medical treatments so far!)* If you're booking your accommodation in advance, then factor in some places that have the right facilities along the way.

Stovetop: Seems to be the key to look for rather than kitchenette when booking accommodation in NZ. Having looked up the meaning of a kitchenette it says: Small cooking area, which usually has a fridge and a microwave, can sometimes have a hotplate and less frequently a sink – so there you go.

When you do your shopping make sure you buy a sharp knife; these are blunt for one of three reasons: 1) In case the guests have annoyed each other and if they haven't got any sharp weapons they are unlikely to kill each other. 2) Most motels don't want you cooking things with strong smells e.g. fish – so a blunt knife isn't going to be of much use preparing fish or meat. 3) They never check if they have gone blunt.

My tip for your cases would be to not put things away when you're only staying for a few nights, and also check the bedsheets! Amazing what can get lost when you chuck things on the bed during your stay.

Transport...

Fuel – use the one that says plus. This is normal unleaded. *(Obviously depending on your car.)* Fill up when you see a petrol station as it's a fair distance between some of them. Chris used his card to pay for petrol on the 2nd March. It showed as a $200 minus on his WeSwap card but did not come off the balance. This is like a holding amount until the transaction has gone through. On the 13th March and it still hasn't applied the $60.49 for petrol we bought and removed the holding fee. *(It never did!)* If we didn't know about this, we could have spent the cash on the card and then when they finally reconciled the amounts, Chris would have got charged for going over on his card balance. Something to be aware of, and why we got two cards from different companies.

Christchurch airport – Once you've checked-in, if you want a bit more choice on the food front then don't go straight through security. There are not as many options, although the café is nice and does amazing sweet potato fries! Fries aside though, we thought there would be more past security but the choice for food is limited. As a bonus we got a meal on the flight from Christchurch to Sydney, with it only being a 3 and half hour flight we didn't think we'd get one. As with all the international flights they have a great selection of films to watch and the seats are comfortable and there is free alcohol.

NZ: Jumping on the fast ferry in the Bay of Islands means you beat the crowds on the main ferry to Russell Island. You don't miss out on any views or the trip; it just means you arrive on Russell Island quicker and have more time before you catch the main boat for your trip.

Milford Sound: Book one of the morning trips as the bus trips haven't arrived. I would say there were fewer than 30 people on our boat. Go for the MV Sinbad, which is one of the smaller ones, as it means they can get closer to the animals and waterfalls, and fewer people, means everyone has room and it's easier to get them all important pictures. They also do free teas and coffees which is a bonus, and they have food you can buy on board.

Toll roads in NZ: If you hire a car, make sure you register your car, which is easy via the website – you will then upload the money, the toll automatically takes the cash. If you don't set it up, then the car hire will pay it but charge you extra for paying it for you.

Car Hire: Make sure you take your documents, especially insurance if you've paid up front. Nearly everyone we have had car hire from tries to charge extra, even when you are fully comp. Documents and proof are your friends to avoid extra charges.

Get there early. Bus trips come from places like Auckland generally arrive around lunchtime, so if you can get there earlier you will get a quieter time to experience the breathtaking views and enjoy the whole vibe of the place.

Flights: All seem to be slightly different when you go through security. I've mentioned about having the details of your flight, accommodation and passport for filling in the forms before you land.

Depending where you're travelling from, book three months in advance through LNER to get the best train deals. Car Hire – book as soon as possible – cheaper to go from South island to North island.

Ferry – book in advance as the one we went on was fully booked.

Sydney: The bus company have an app which you can download; this is useful for seeing where the bus stops are located and the rough times. They have two routes – red is the city one and blue is the one for Bondi beach.

Sydney: If you get one of the first buses out, be prepared for the bus driver to be selling the tour tickets to people and advising them; this equals to you hanging about on the bus for a long time. Not every stop has one of the guides on the roadside selling and giving information.

Sydney: If you're not bothered about commentary on the tourist boats, then get an Opal card and use the normal ferries to get around. I think one journey cost us about $3 which is approximately £1.50, and you still get the amazing views of Sydney Opera House and Bridge but fewer tourists and you can just enjoy the views.

Singapore: For international flights you will be given a slip of paper to fill in when you arrive, you hand this over with your passport at security. It asks for name, DOB, where you're staying, how long for and passport number. So, to make life easier, have a pen in your bag and keep your passport and hotel/connecting details to hand so you can fill this in on the plane – just saves a bit of time.

General...

Picton: Stop and get some supplies when you get off the ferry.

Anything you want to do, get there early to avoid any organised trips.

Take a photo on your camera which has your phone number and email address on in case you lose your camera.

Cases: We wondered what to bring as our plan was to do a road trip, and we wanted to make sure we could fit most of the stuff in the boot of the car. We have one medium size case and a carry-on sized suitcase and these fit perfectly in our Suzuki swift car boot along with our two rucksacks. We use a pushbike lock to secure them. To be honest it's not really needed as there doesn't seem to be much crime, but I feel better knowing they are locked up when we park the car up to wander about a place en route to our next stop or stop to take pictures.

NZ Trips: We booked the Te Anau glow worm caves and the Milford Sound boat trip which saves you 20% at the tourist information point in Te Anau.

Clean your boots/shoes before you leave NZ. You will receive a form on all international flights. On the form it asks about wilderness /trekking. There are hefty fines if you mislead or lie so be truthful even if you think you will get delayed. We ticked yes to being in the wilderness – we had been on a road trip and had a rucksack full of walking boots so couldn't claim to have been sunning ourselves on a pristine yacht for the whole time. Anyway, we were sensible, and I cleaned off our boots before we left. While in the line a woman came down and checked the forms before we got to security and we confirmed we'd cleaned them and that was it; she marked it okay and off we went. Better to have a delay. You wouldn't want to be responsible for bringing in something you shouldn't or the fine.

Suncream: Make sure you read the instructions and rub it in!

Sandfly repellent: Buy as much as you can afford if you're susceptible to bites! Mainly in the South – could be a time of year kind of thing but take some just in case. Also, wear a onesie or spacesuit on the Westcoast; you might look daft, but you will be the one laughing when you have no bites.

Sydney: For those struggling with data you can also get free Wi-Fi in the Botanical Gardens.

Money...

Get an LYK Card. I read some negative reviews about the LYK card, but it worked perfectly on contactless, in the ATMs and the pending activity for a payment shows straight away so useful for keeping track of what you've spent on the app. *(Obviously since I've written this Thomas Cook went bust but the Lyk cards are owned by a different company. Just make sure you get a card where the transactions show immediately.)*

Money – we checked all the options, and we decided to cover all bases, so we applied for a credit card that had free international purchases for the accommodation. I got a Lyk card from Thomas Cook. I went into the shop, and they upload the money and convert it at this time. You can then draw out/use contactless as a standard card when abroad. Chris decided to go with a WeSwap card which does the same thing. We'd read some stories about people having problems. Touch wood, we had no significant issues other than the fuel. We have both drawn money out, paid for items in supermarkets and they worked fine for the most part. My personal opinion is that the Lyk worked better than the WeSwap card. When you want more money in a particular currency you merely transfer the cash from the bank you have it linked to. Be aware though as they say it can take up to seven days to show on your card. So, think about this if transferring when abroad. Although, it was immediate when we transferred money.

Cash withdrawals – try and find a bank with free withdrawals. We used one in a shopping centre and got charged Singapore $8.70/£5 in bank charges.

Contactless Payment is available in most places – they call it Paywave in NZ.

Singapore: Has a chilled tax of $0.15 on bottled drinks.

Daily spends

	Dollars	UK
Day 1		£33
56 SGD to £1		
Day 2	$32.20	£18.00
Day 3	$142.95	£80.00
Day 4	$94.40	£53.00
52 NZD to £1		
Day 5	$106.38	£55
Day 6	$174.05	£91
Day 7	$150.84	£78
Day 8	$103.62	£54
Day 9	$71.50	£37
Day 10	$321.32	£167
Day 11	$172.46	£90
Day 12	$400.47	£208
Day 13	$77.59	£40
Day 14	$146.79	£76
Day 15	$184.28	£96
Day 16	$90.53	£47
Day 17	$55.87	£29

	Dollars	UK
Day 18	$151.47	£79
Day 19	$105.41	£55
Day 20	$677.15	£352
Day 21	$111.74	£58
Day 22	$110.00	£57
Day 23	$216.96	£113
Day 24	$99.25	£52
Day 25	$282.74	£147
Day 26	$289.90	£151
Day 27	$58.90	£31
Day 28	$228.31	£119
Day 29	$198.53	£103
Day 30	$125.28	£65
Day 31	$157.67	£82
Day 32	$54.50	£28
Day 33	$160.44	£83

0.54 dollar to UK

	Dollars	UK
Day 33	$85.53	£46
Day 34	$405.94	£219
Day 35	$82.59	£45

	Dollars	UK
Day 36	$141.90	£77
Day 37	$294.35	£159
Day 38	$188.37	£102
Day 39	$156.36	£85
Day 40	$53.70	£29
56 SGD to £1		
Day 40	$41.23	£23
Day 41	$127.90	£72
Day 42	$31.80	£18 £12
Day 43		£20
Total Spent:	UK	**£3734**

Other costs

New Zealand		Holiday gifts	$18.20
Sim cards x2	$58.00	Bus trip Auckland	$38.00
Cool bag	$8.00	Taxi airport	$35.00
Toll Roads	$5.22	Ferry - prepaid	£139.00
Ice packs	$4.00	Bay of Islands boat x2	$201.60

Gifts car boot	$5.00	Hobbiton movie tour x2	$168.00
Lock	$6.00	Helicopter ride x2	$550.00
Insect spray	$9.45	Museum x2 Terracotta warriors	$39.99
Sun cream	$10.00	Fjordlands Cinema x2	$20.00
Plastic cutlery	$0.59	Glow worm caves x2	$174.00
Scissors	$2.00	Milford Sound Boat Cruise	$174.00
Tupperware	$2.70	Cablecar wellingtonx2	$18.00
Stamps	$2.40	Gondola Queenstown	$78.00
Trip to Doctors	$177.00	Rail trip Dunedin x2	$120.00
Sudafed	$20.99	Wildlife Park Christchurch	$65.00
Lemsips	£12.99	Cough sweets	$2.09
Blue Mountains bus tour Sydney	£86.50	Hop on Hop off Sydney including boat/Sydney tower	£112.00

Food costs if you really want them...

I might not have added everything as I may not want to admit to any cakes...

> **TOP TIP:** *Great savings if you get a New World tourist discount card*

New Zealand Dollars			
Water 750ml	2.00	Paper towel x2	2.00
Bluebird crisps 10pk	3.49	Vegetable Frittata deli	2.97
Mainland feta 200g	3.30	Salad Thai kumara	3.89
Baby lettuce 100g	3.50	Pilsner 6pk 330ml	10.99
Ciabatta cobs	1.19	Hummus 175g	3.00
Gala Apple	0.36	Milk lite 1l	2.30
Tomato	0.41	Veggiburger 4pk 500g	6.00
Premium coleslaw 100g	1.66	Curry vegi selection box	20.50
Beetroot and feta salad 100g deli	2.55	Greek salad 100g deli counter	4.42
Victoria bitter 6pack	13.99	Coffee sachets	4.00
Crinkle cut crisps 10pk	3.00	Rice crackers	1.99
Falafel bites 340g	6.99	Cling film 60 m	3.00

Item	Price	Item	Price
Bread roll baguettes	3.79	Crispy Salad 300g	3.99
Coconut curry sauce	2.49	Smoked cheese 200g	4.50
Noodles x2	2.19	Monteith's beer 6 pak	13.99
Soya bean oil	1.99	Milk standard 300ml	1.24
Wok frozen vegetables	5.19	Weet-bix cereal	3.49
Toui IPA Beer 12pk 330ml	17.99	Double express cold coffee	3.49
Rolls x4	2.89	Golden crumpets 6 pk	2.85
1 tomato	0.48	Pasta fettuccine	1.99
One onion	0.36	McCain mixed veg	3.19
Rose fizz	5.99	Premium pasta sauce	2.49
Kellogg's cornflakes 380G	2.95	Bean supreme veggie sausages x6	8.29
Spinach & feta Humous	3.39	Cooked roast beef slices	3.12
Packet cappas x10	2.99	Uncle ben egg rice fried	2.00
Sugar 550g	1.29	Pams soy sauce 300ml	1.59
English Muffins	3.85	Mushrooms .18 kg	2.34
Mini baguettes x4	2.89	Gala apples x2	2.17

Item	Price	Item	Price
Nut bar deluxe 210g	2.99	Mac hop rocker 330ml x6	15.99
Golden crumpets x6	1.99	Free range eggs x6	4.95
Kellogg's corn flakes	3.49	Mushrooms 0.135kg	1.75
Salted popcorn 80g	2.49	Dry roasted peanuts 200g	2.49
Lindauer Pinot Gris x4	17.99	Feta sundried tomato 150g	4.29
Crunchie bar 50g	1.29	Veg Malaysian tofu 200g	4.90
Pumpkin/feta lasagna	5.99	Thai fish cakes 320G x4	8.19
Chips crinkle x10	3.19	Cinnamon Pinwheel	2.69
Red pepper	2.09	Cooper pale ale 750ml	5.99
Watties tomato sauce 330g	3.00		
Sydney			
Chips chunky 1kg	2.00	Bertolli butter spread 400g	3.80
Tomatoes 250gm	4.00	Peppermint tea 40pk	1.75
X6 Coopers green	21.99	Moccona café 10pk	4.50
sliced beetroot 415g	2.50	cottage cheese 500g	2.90
Peeled tomatoes 400g	.80	Muffins 6 pack	2.50

Peeled tomatoes 400g	.80		Muffins 6 pack	2.50
Red pepper 0.187	1.85		Doritos 170g	1.64
Onion 0.152kg	0.61		Garlic bread 300g	4.00
Sliced mushrooms	4.00		Dolmio pasta sauce 500g	3.30
Kitkat triple choc	2.00		Eggs 12	3.60

Accommodation Costs

	Nights	Accommodation	Cost
Singapore	2	Furama Riverside	£214.96
Auckland	2	Quest on Eden	£176.64
Pukenui	2	Pukenui Lodge Motel	£125.39
Whangerai	2	Discovery settlers Hotel	£133.06
Rotorua	2	Geneva Motor Lodge	£157.97
Napier	1	BK Fountain Court	£70.16
Wellington	2	Marksman Motor Inn	£163.01
Murchison	1	Mataki Hotel	£64.36
Karamea	1	Last Resort Karamea	£67.05

	Nights	Accommodation	Cost
Greymouth	1	Greymouth Kiwi Holiday Park and motel	£78.24
Franz Josef	1	Glacier View Motel	£78.20
Haast	1	Asure Aspiring Court Motel	£85.42
Wanaka	1	Golfcourse Road Chalets and Lodge	£99.45
Queenstown	1	Garden Court Suites	£98.15
Te Anau	4	Parklands Motel	£294.98
Dunedin	2	Leith Valley Holiday Park and Motels	£144.00
Christchurch	4	South Brighton Holiday park	£226.00
Sydney	7	Buxton House	£512.89
Singapore	2	Destination Hotel	£186.00
UK	1	Ibis	£55.00
		Total Cost	**£3030.93**

Fuel costs

Cost per litre	Litres	Price
2.09	27	$57.75
2.02	31,6	$64,20
2.02	32.74	$66.43
2.02	29.96	$60.79
2.06	21.39	$44.04
2.23	29.42	$65.85
2.32	31.44	$72.95
2.29	25.20	$56.17
2.18	13.05	$28.57
2.15	35.08	$76.98
2,15	34.70	$74.90
2.15	37.29	$80.50
Mileage 635/394		**$749.13**
	UK	£390

Total spent on our 43-day adventure...

Accommodation Costs	£3030.93
Spends (including fuel)	£3734.00
Flights booked through Trail Finders – 6 flights in total	£2100.00
Train tickets to London return	£28.00
Car Hire	£591.00
Ferry	£139.00
Other items (luggage, clothes etc)	£300.00
Insurance	£100.00
Total Costs	**£10022.93**

£10022.93 over 43 days is **£233 per day**.

Now this really is the end… if you're planning an adventure, I hope you love it as much as we did.

Happy Travelling xx

Printed in Poland
by Amazon Fulfillment
Poland Sp. z o.o., Wrocław